CROWD AND MASS BEHAVIOR

READINGS IN SOCIOLOGY SERIES

ALLYN AND BACON, INC.
Boston • Rockleigh, N.J.
Atlanta • Dallas • Belmont, Calif.

CROWD AND MASS BEHAVIOR

Compiled and edited by
Helen MacGill Hughes, Ph.D.

SOCIOLOGICAL RESOURCES FOR THE SOCIAL STUDIES
Sponsored by the American Sociological Association
Supported by the National Science Foundation

April 1972
Copyright © 1972 by the American Sociological Association. All rights reserved.

Crowd and Mass Behavior is one of a series of books and other materials prepared by Sociological Resources for the Social Studies for use in the schools. SRSS is sponsored by the American Sociological Association and supported by the National Science Foundation.

Printed in the United States of America
Library of Congress Catalog Card Number 73–186410

Foreword

The "what is" of the social world is of primary interest to the sociologist. He wants to know about existing patterns of human relationships, why they are as they are (their causes), and what consequences they have for people, groups, and society in general (their effects). But to find out what, in fact, these patterns of relationships are, the sociologist must study society itself. He must conduct research on group behavior, studying how various groups are related to one another and to the institutions of society.

Take, for example, the militant political groups of young people that sprang up in the late sixties. The sociologist tries to understand the conditions and events in society generally and the experiences in family, school, and peer groups that have led the members of these groups to organize and establish their programs of activities. He also seeks to discover the effects of such activities on universities, communities, and political life in the whole society. Thus his research into a particular kind of group adds to knowledge about other groups and institutions and how they function in society.

Because research plays such a major role in learning about our society, it is important that various research studies on a particular topic be brought together in one place so that we may have a more comprehensive picture of that topic. *Crowd and Mass Behavior* is a book of such research studies. It is made up of a set of readings that present in clear language the results of important sociological research. Studies on which the readings are based were done by competent social scientists, and each volume in this *Readings in Sociology* Series therefore presents significant information in its field.

The selections included in each volume not only present research results but also reveal the methods used by investigators to obtain those results. By studying these volumes and other materials described below, students can learn what social scientists do and how they do it.

The *Readings in Sociology* Series is one part of a three-part program known as the SRSS Program developed by the curriculum project Sociological Resources for the Social Studies (an agency of the American Sociological Association) and published by Allyn and Bacon, Inc. Another part of the program is the *Episodes in Social Inquiry* Series, which consists of a large number of short units called episodes that are suitable for use in a variety of social studies courses. Each has a more specific topic than any of the volumes of readings, and each is designed for an inquiry mode of learning.

The third part of the SRSS program is an introductory sociology course, *Inquiries in Sociology*. This course aims to give a sound basis in sociology while treating topics especially relevant to student interests. As with the episodes, there are exercises designed to stimulate the curiosity of students and give them practice in social investigation.

Many distinguished sociologists have worked in collaboration with high school teachers in designing and writing materials for the project. The central staff has seen these materials through the long process of national trial, evaluation, and revision.

The SRSS materials are suitable for use in a variety of social studies courses where they can enhance the existing curriculum by adding a sociological perspective. For example, in addition to use in sociology courses, the materials may be easily integrated into such courses as history, problems of democracy, civics, social problems, economics, and political science. In addition, some materials are well suited for such courses as English, mathematics, psychology, family life, and the humanities.

The aim of the SRSS project has been to provide materials which are relevant to the interests and concerns of students and which afford them an understanding of sociological concepts and methods at work.

Robert C. Angell

Preface

Do people in a crowd do things they would not do by themselves?

Is the behavior of people in a crowd—a panic or a riot, for example—always unpredictable and unique? Or does it follow some sort of pattern?

How do people come to act in the same way without actually meeting or communicating with each other?

Does such behavior (mass behavior) follow rules?

Does a social movement like Women's Liberation have anything in common with other movements, for example, Black Power?

When some strong sentiment on a public question leads people to form an organization, can the organization survive when the issue has changed? If so, what must the organization do to survive?

Unorganized behavior is the subject of this book. The first selection tells how the sociologist goes about studying it, what he looks for, and what methods he uses to find the facts he needs in order to understand it better. This is followed by a selection which describes the many forms unorganized behavior may take. The remaining 18 selections are a display of some of these forms. *The readings do not offer a complete survey of unorganized behavior. Instead, each selection was chosen as a statement of interesting research on some aspect of unorganized behavior.*

The selection on the generation gap (the third reading) draws attention to the fact of "polarization"—to use a word which has lately become very popular—and shows that age is not the only basis on which people take sides on questions of the day. The many divisions of public opinion and the ways in which they affect individuals are examined further in the account of how people decide which way to vote in elections (selection eight).

Crowd behavior, another form of unorganized behavior, may occur when people are together and can see and hear each other.

The ninth, fourteenth, sixteenth, and seventeenth selections are studies of the social interaction among people face to face. Selection seven, a case on social contagion, presents a not very common form of the spread of a response to a situation. Here an hysterical rash afflicted only those who were in communication with each other. Thus the route of their social interaction is highly visible.

In selections ten to thirteen and eighteen to twenty, social movements are presented. Social movements today are often on a very large scale and have become normal aspects of daily life. Much behavior that used to be wholly private has now become public and political. Witness, for example, the Women's Liberation Movement, which before our eyes is transforming domestic concerns into matters for pressure groups, petitions, appeals to Congressmen, union leaders, church authorities, and the like. The management of the family and the careers of women are only one instance. The governing of universities and the private life of the clergy have become subjects on which laymen are beginning to have opinions and to demand a hearing. Corresponding to this development the sociologists are focusing attention on social movements, who is attracted to them, and what becomes of the movements.

Social movements often involve crowd behavior, and in many cases they give rise to organizations. Out of the youth movement of the late 1960s have come the Students for a Democratic Society (SDS), the radical Weathermen, and many other societies. Thousands upon thousands of students who join in sit-ins and demonstrations do not actually become members of the organizations devoted to protest. Organizations, with their leaders, executive committees, stated purposes, and codes of rules, involve quite another type of interaction.*

There is, besides public opinion and social movements, the type of unorganized interaction called mass behavior. Here individuals respond to a situation in the same way—but one by one, and not by united action. Mass behavior is represented in this book in several readings. The fourth selection reports how the people of the United States reacted in their homes, offices, fac-

---

* See *Social Organizations* in this *Readings in Sociology* Series.

tories, schools, or on the street, when they heard the shocking news of the death of President Kennedy. The fifth reading examines the mechanism by which one member of the mass comes to act in the same way as another. Other studies of the mass are described in the readings on fashion (six) and on hero worship (fifteen).

The questions which precede each selection are ones which the author of the research hoped to answer by his studies. They are not intended as questions to be put to the student.

At the end of the book is a list of selected readings, keyed by number to the selections on which they have a bearing.

Sociological Resources for the Social Studies gratefully acknowledges advice and suggestions for this book from the following scholars: Herbert Blumer, Allan Eister, Arlie Hochschild, Herbert Hyman, Elihu Katz, Gladys Engel Lang, Gary T. Marx, John Spiegel, and Ralph H. Turner.

It also gratefully acknowledges permission kindly given by the following publications and publishers to adapt selections for the book: *American Anthropologist, American Journal of Sociology, American Scholar, American Sociological Review, Annals of the American Academy of Political and Social Science,* Barnes and Noble, Inc., Columbia University Press, *Human Organization, Journal of Social Issues, New Society, Public Opinion Quarterly, Ramparts,* Simon and Schuster, *Social Problems, Sociological Quarterly, Sociometry.*

It acknowledges, too, the services of the following writers who adapted selections: Warren Breed, James Cornell, Eleanor Gates, Sally Martin, and the editorial services of Nancy Stein Seasholes.

Contents

Sociologists Look at Crowd and Mass Behavior*

Why does a class of students, a street crowd, or an audience suddenly get out of control?

How is it that apparently carefree students unexpectedly turn into campus protesters?

How can large numbers of people all nearly at the same time fall ill from "poisoned water" when the water has definitely not been poisoned?

Sociologists are fascinated by and curious about crowd and mass behavior because the causes, the course such behavior runs, and its consequences are often hard to determine. They study the Watts riot or the hippie movement because they are trying to understand these important events and processes. Moreover, sociologists also find in these instances of crowd and mass behavior a natural laboratory for studying some basic aspects of social interaction and organization.

In this book you will read about the ways in which people come to grips with unusual, puzzling, troublesome, or threatening events and changes in the world around them. Sometimes they respond, as Herbert Blumer explains, as a *mass* with many persons in different places responding to the same event. This happened, for instance, at the time of the assassination of President Kennedy ("Americans in a Time of Crisis") and on the occasion of the first televised debate between two candidates for the Presidency ("The Making of the President: 1940 and 1960"). Other events to which people respond as a mass are new inventions ("How New Ideas Spread") and new fashions ("Fashion: The Rhythm of Change").

---

* Written for this book by Gladys Engel Lang.

Sometimes people gather together in *crowds*. They walk about listening to rumors to find out what is happening ("The Riot That Didn't Happen"), or they riot against their lot in life ("Watts: Who Rioted and Why"). Faced by what they believe to be certain disaster, people may flee ("When Disaster Strikes") or may become hysterically ill ("The Spread of a Social Contagion"). At still other times people who are troubled by events near at home or far away may gather together in peaceful assembly to demonstrate their protest: they stage boycotts ("War Toys and the Peace Movement"), or they march for peace ("The Peace Marchers") or for the liberation of women ("The Women's Liberation Movement").

In reading this book, you will also find how opinions form and change in response to events. The *public,* as Blumer explains, is made up of the people who are concerned over the same issue and have an opinion about it. They express their opinions in discussion with others. People may rally to the support of someone they idolize ("Hero Worship") or they may divide into camps, as they do when making up their minds how to vote in an election ("The Making of the President: 1940 and 1960"). When young people and their elders look at the same events but view them quite differently, you have what Ann Brunswick speaks of as a "real" generation gap. She regards the young and the old as two publics, where opinions, not age, are the important difference separating the two groups.

People whose attitudes and values are very different from the majority sometimes withdraw into a world of their own. This is true of the hippies whom John Howard describes here. Groups of like-minded people may join in *social movements* to bring about changes they want, as did the black nationalists whom Blake studied. Such social movements occur among the politically left ("The Student Protesters") and the politically right ("The Radical Right"). The old and poor may organize for economic security during their retirement, and temperance crusaders may band together to stop others from drinking intoxicating beverages ("Two Social Movements and Their Fates"). Some social movements fail to acquire wide popular support and die out without changing anything; other social movements gain their goals and then either disappear or set new goals.

COLLECTIVE BEHAVIOR

Crowd and mass behavior—the subject of the selections in this book—are studied by sociologists who work in a field called *collective behavior*. The type of behavior these sociologists study is in some ways, but not all ways, similar to behavior in organized groups, as for example, a factory, a church, or a school class. Both unorganized and organized behavior involve problem-solving, but there is a difference.

In organized groups each person has a place; he is given a job and usually knows what is expected of him when certain problems arise. These routines of everyday life in institutions—on the job, in the home, or in school—have grown up in response to situations that people have to cope with repeatedly, perhaps even every day. The routines are the "answers" that everybody is expected to learn; as long as the answers "work," the routines are usually accepted as rules of behavior. Yet people often find themselves in problematic situations where they are not sure exactly what they are expected to do or where they do not really want to obey the rules or simply fall in with what others think. If the situation is so unusual or so trying that many people cannot cope with it routinely, then it is even more problematic. Therefore, because no one knows just what is to be done, there may be unexpected behavior and new solutions.

Behavior that develops in response to problematic situations is called *collective* behavior. It is different from the more routinized kind of problem-solving called *social* behavior in three ways: It is *less inhibited;* it is *more changeable;* and it is *shorter-lived.*

Less inhibited? This means that people act more spontaneously. In a crowd, people give way more easily to emotions they ordinarily hold back; they share the mood of the moment. They may weep, scream, or laugh wildly—all because everybody else seems to be doing so. A member of the public, though normally shy, may feel called upon to speak his own mind. A participant in a social movement will do things in order to air a grievance—like carrying a sign in a parade or meeting with the mayor—that he would never dare to do, or even think of doing, by himself.

More changeable? Behavior is more likely to change form

and direction quickly. People, seeking a way out of confusion, will turn wherever they can for guidance about what to think and how to act. They talk to people they ordinarily would not talk to or listen to. New leaders appear who gain followers because they put into words feelings which people have vaguely felt. Today we are witnessing the rise of new leaders, for example, the blacks and the Women's Liberation Movement. Alan Kerckhoff and his fellow social psychologists illustrate, as does Elihu Katz, how people accept suggestions from others whose behavior they copy or whose ideas they adopt. In this way new forms of behavior that ordinarily would not be thought of gain acceptance—like the looting (which is reported here in the study of the Watts riot) by some of the rioters.

Shorter-lived? Crowds and mass movements usually spring to life quickly and disappear quickly as well. How long can an agitator hold the interest of a crowd? How long can politicians maintain the people's attention during a campaign? How long can the enthusiasm displayed by the pioneers of a new social movement last? Crowds, by nature, disappear. They break up as individuals go back to other things which claim their attention. In order to last, they must become organized.

But if the crowd organizes, it is no longer a crowd. In the same ways, when publics organize themselves, they become pressure groups, or if they organize in support of some "idol," they become fan clubs. Social movements, like the Townsendites studied by Sheldon Messinger and the antiliquor forces studied by Joseph Gusfield, usually become voluntary associations.

WHY STUDY CROWD AND MASS BEHAVIOR?

What first attracted sociologists at the beginning of this century to the study of mass and crowd behavior was the unusual manner in which people sometimes behaved when together in large numbers. Some acted as if they were psychologically intoxicated, conducting themselves in ways very different from the ordinary. More important, the behavior of these few, however strange, appeared then to be picked up and to spread in an epidemic-like fashion. Early sociologists looked at crowd and mass behavior as a throwback to barbarism.

4

Today, sociologists know that people—in panic, looting, rumormongering, and so forth—behave in ways neither so unusual nor so mysterious as had once been believed. People do not usually become completely irrational and irresponsible. Enrico Quarantelli points out that you do not have to be out of your mind to flee in panic, for sometimes running away is the most sensible way of avoiding being caught in disaster. The articles on riots show that rioting is, for one thing, a way of calling attention to social injustice when authorities seem to reject protests.

Other forms of collective behavior, such as social movements, which are more organized, offer the sociologist a chance to study the nature of leadership. In particular he seeks to learn how people become leaders, how leaders replace one another, how they influence their followers, and how leaders are in turn influenced by followers.

Finally, there is a more practical reason for studying crowd and mass behavior. Riots, as well as the campus and street demonstrations described in this book, arouse strong and divided feelings among nonparticipants, with each side developing its own myths. Ralph Conant describes two myths about the Watts riot. The one held by most blacks was that of a "group protest over genuine grievances" while the one believed by most whites was that of "criminal behavior of riffraff." Where there is such wide disagreement, careful investigation by research experts who have no ax to grind can help set the record straight.

Findings from sociological research on crowds have also guided police officials in preventing riots and in halting, without bloodshed, riots already under way. For this reason, some people, including some sociologists, fear that research may possibly become a tool for blocking legitimate protest. Still, by setting the facts straight, sociological research, like the study of rioting, helps to dispel some popular misunderstandings. David Sears and John McConahay in their study showed that most Watts rioters were not riffraff but respectable poor people with many economic and social grievances. Whereas sensational newspaper accounts and television coverage tend to single out the violence associated with peace protest, sociological studies, like that of the Peace Marchers in London, document how completely nonviolent is the behavior of most participants during most demonstrations.

In this respect, sociologists set the record straight for future historians as well. It is interesting to note that for almost two centuries school children have learned that the storming of the Bastille during the French Revolution was the act of a howling, criminal mob of riffraff. Analysis based on official records of those arrested or known to have participated now shows that most of the rioters came from the immediately surrounding community and were respectable, employed workingmen. Well-documented events occurring today may help prevent the growth and spread of similar misinterpretations.

METHODS OF STUDY

Sociologists must try to organize their research in advance if they want to observe collective behavior as it happens. Where they can anticipate a problematic situation to which people will have to react—as in the case of an election or a massive demonstration—they can organize a team of observers well ahead of time. This is what the sociologists studying the peace marchers and the voters' responses to electoral campaigns did. To study unexpected events like disasters that occur suddenly and without advance warning requires teams of observers or interviewers who are prepared to move in as soon as authorities allow, like those with whom Quarantelli worked.

Other sociologists observe on their own—as individuals. Often they become observers of situations in which they happen to be present. They are able to see more than many others because of the skill they have acquired through training. Their familiarity with the studies already made of collective behavior alerts them to significant clues that others might easily overlook. But they must also familiarize themselves with the particular situation being studied. They become participant observers by attending meetings, getting to know participants, being on the scene. In that way John Howard, for instance, studied the San Francisco hippies. Richard Flacks studied student protesters at the university where he taught. J. Herman Blake observed the black nationalists.

There are, however, other methods besides observation. Many of the studies reviewed in this book used surveys, with teams of interviewers asking people the same questions about their opinions and behavior. For instance, Paul Sheatsley and Jacob Feldman used a survey to find out about public reaction to the news of President Kennedy's assassination. Ann Brunswick's analysis of the generation gap made use of information from a number of surveys. Repeated interviewing of the same group of voters—called a panel survey—was used in Paul Lazarsfeld's study of decision-making in the 1940 Presidential election and in the Langs' investigation of televiewers' reactions to the Kennedy-Nixon debates in 1960. Elihu Katz and also Alan Kerckhoff and his associates, used survey responses to make a sociometric analysis. This is a technique for plotting statistically the networks of friendship and communication through which ideas spread.

In some cases where events can be studied only after they are past, the sociologist is forced to rely on information provided by others, such as newspaper accounts, official reports, or other documents. Orrin Klapp's work on hero worship is based on the analysis of such materials. So is A. L. Kroeber's study of changes in fashion. Some research depends upon the availability of statistical records. Sociologists studying the Watts riot analyzed statistically the background characteristics of persons arrested at the time. Marlene Dixon's review of the Women's Liberation Movement is, in large part, based on analysis of statistics of the labor force.

Many studies of collective behavior make use of a combination of methods in order to get a more complete view of a single event. The sociologist studying rapidly changing events has to be flexible and ready to use whatever methods fit the case. He has to come close enough to whatever he is studying to get the feel of it but not so close that "he cannot see the forest for the trees."

A crowd is always in flux, and the sociologist must not mistake what goes on at any one point in it for what the crowd is in its totality. For a crowd consists of a great many different people: it consists not only of those in its forefront but also those far in its background. It includes leaders and instigators, timid followers, curious bystanders, and even those who observe only from a distance over television. A true view of the crowd takes in those trying to restrain its actions—perhaps the police—and those actively opposing it. Thus what the sociologist calls *the* crowd is only the result of what goes on between all these people. Likewise, the character and influence of a social movement depends not only on who its leaders and followers are but also on who its opponents are.

How does the sociologist proceed in studying such complicated events? He begins by collecting information, looking at what happened from every possible angle, and checking through every report. From all the information he has gathered, by whatever method, he then tries to reconstruct a picture of what really happened. Next, he interprets his data to see how they fit in with what is generally known about crowd and mass behavior, testing to see if his findings confirm, modify, or refute his own ideas and the findings of others. From all this he finally formulates a theory of what generally happens under such circumstances. Such a theory depends, of course, on accurate information, but its ultimate worth is a product of creative imagination. That is to say, he must use intuition to grasp in his mind how and why people respond to the various types of problematic situations in the particular ways they do.

Research on crowd and mass behavior is, for the sociologist, a high risk undertaking. All his planning and efforts may prove in vain. The characteristics of collective behavior which have been mentioned—its impulsiveness, unpredictability, and changeability—make this kind of research tricky. Events have a way of happening and being over before a sociologist can get into the field. Thus, young people were hippie dropouts and women were already well into what is now called the Women's Liberation Movement long before these movements came to public attention. Indeed, social movements usually gain attention only if they are successful and/or have reached a stage of organization at which they can hardly be ignored. By the time you read this book, many of the movements mentioned will have changed. Some may even have been forgotten along with their heroes. Heroes, as everyone knows, are often heroes only for a day.

Forms of Crowd and
Mass Behavior*

People in human society have many occasions to act without following what is laid down by regulations, laws, customs, or established ways. What are the major types of such new shared behavior? How is each developed?

What is the difference in behavior and outcome between people who act either (a) under the impact of shared and heightened emotion, (b) as a result of argument about issues that confront them, or (c) as separate individuals in response to appeals that are addressed to them in the mass?

What are the mechanisms in the formation of social movements that explain why such movements grow, survive, or perish?

"We bombed out in the semifinals, so we had all day Sunday to wander around the campus," Harry said.

He was telling Charlie after school about the school band's trip to the band contest at State College. Harry went on: "Well, they were having something called an Ecology Teach-in there and it was really something. It was about things like pollution and the environment. They were saying that unless we do something about automobiles, we'll all die of suffocation within ten years. And if we don't watch out we're going to bury ourselves in garbage. Either that, or have so much to burn that we'll suffocate from the smoke. And they showed slides and diagrams of the water we drink—ugh! It was awful!"

By this time several others had joined Harry and Charlie. They all had seen programs on television about the pollution problem. Each tried to tell some grim tale he had heard about

* Adapted from "Collective Behavior" by Herbert Blumer, in *Principles of Sociology*, Alfred McClung Lee, ed. (New York: Barnes and Noble, Inc., 1969), pp. 67–120. Reprinted by permission.

the pollution of air, land, and water. Then Charlie spoke. "We're in bad shape. We ought to do something about it; not just stand around and gripe."

"I know," said Harry. "We ought to go to City Hall and demand they clean these things up."

"No. They won't listen to a bunch of kids," said Estelle Jones, editor of the school paper. "What we should do is write a letter to the editor." Seeing several friends nod their heads in agreement, she added, "Then everybody will read about it."

Again they were all talking at once, taking sides, arguing, criticizing officials, suggesting reforms. Soon about 30 more students had joined the discussion. Very little was settled in the way of a plan of action. But from the point of view of a sociologist who studies collective behavior, a great deal had been happening.

The students were dissatisfied with waste and pollution. But what then? No one was acknowledged as leader or given any responsibilities. Moreover, they had no clear idea of what immediate or future steps would be necessary to launch a campaign against pollution.

How different this situation is from organized behavior! Take Harry's band, for example. It was a marvel of planned regulation. Each boy knew exactly what was expected of him, from playing the notes exactly as written to marching in well-rehearsed formation. The conductor was boss, the first trumpets played the lead, the tubas provided the "oom-pahs" at the proper moment, the clarinets skirled in classic fashion. Common understandings, traditions, expectations, rules, and routines dictated what each was to do. This is social organization. It is far different from that random and spontaneous talk about ecology and pollution after school—which sociologists classify as an instance of "collective behavior."

All social behavior is collective and to call only certain cases of it collective is not logical. However, in the various forms of collective behavior, such as crowds, mobs, hysterias, manias, fashions, fads, demonstrations, and public opinion, it is clear that although the activity is not organized, individuals nevertheless are strongly influenced by others. Collective behavior is at the very opposite pole from institutions and organizations.* This area of social behavior has been analyzed by Professor Herbert Blumer of the University of California at Berkeley. The definitions and descriptions in the pages which follow are taken from his writings.

ELEMENTARY FORMS OF COLLECTIVE BEHAVIOR

When the individuals in a community are made restless by some object or situation that seems to disturb them all, their behavior may take new and strange, yet typical, forms. These are elementary collective mechanisms: milling, collective excitement, and social contagion. They are elementary because they appear spontaneously, rather than being staged or planned in advance. They are the simplest and earliest ways in which people collectively express unrest and they usually lead to more complicated interaction.

The basic type of the elementary forms is *milling*. Individuals move among one another in aimless fashion, like sheep in a moment of excitement. The effect of milling is to make each more sensitive to the others. The reaction becomes circular, that is, the persons who stimulate you are then stimulated by you. Thus the process is intensified. As the individuals grow increasingly preoccupied with one another they become less responsive to everyday stimuli. (The same state is seen, in more exaggerated form, in hypnosis.) Being preoccupied with each other, they all are more inclined to respond to each other quickly, directly, and unwittingly. Then they are ready to act *as a group*. It is not uncommon for students to mill in the corridors or the campus when an unpopular new rule is announced.

An even more intensive form of milling is *collective excitement*. The individual—call him John Doe—rivets his attention on Richard Roe and others in the crowd and on the excitement they display. John thus becomes less able to check his actions by reference to facts. Under the influence of collective excitement he may then embark on lines of conduct which previously he would have scorned.

* See "Organizations, Associations, and Institutions" and "The Function of Ritual in an Organization" in *Social Organizations* in this *Readings in Sociology* Series.

The most extreme form of such behavior follows upon *social contagion.** This refers to the rapid and nonrational growth of a mood or impulse as in crazes, manias, fads, financial panics, and war hysterias. These are all occasions when rumors spread rapidly and quite sensible people believe and pass on to others wild and irresponsible statements which they normally would ignore.

The social contagion reaches John Doe. Bystanders and indifferent spectators may be swept into the crowd. As they catch the spirit of excitement, their attention becomes more sharply focused and their resistance weakens. Some seem to lose their critical ability. They then are open to the impulse of the group. Given the proper conditions this behavior will "spread like wildfire," as in cases of an orgy of speculation, a financial panic, a lynching, or a wave of patriotic hysteria.

THE CROWD

Most scholars identify four types of crowd: the casual crowd, the conventionalized crowd, the acting crowd, and the expressive crowd. To give examples: The *casual crowd* forms and dissolves, as when numbers of people visit a park, a market center, or a museum. The *conventionalized crowd* may be the audience at a track meet or at the theater. On such occasions the crowd knows the expected ways of acting, such as cheering or applauding.

The *acting crowd* starts with an exciting event which catches the attention of many. They grow restless because they do not know what to do. Milling will be the first preparation for action: John Doe becomes aware of the excitement shown by others. As the contagion intensifies he begins to respond, without reflecting, to the remarks and actions of others. He will act now, rather than after deliberate thought. In short, he is highly suggestible now.

Eventually the impulses, feelings, and imagery of the people will become focused on some object of common attention. It may be the event in which the excitement originated or it may be some common complaint that emerges from the milling and talking. At any rate, the people now share a goal and are in a position to act with unity and purpose.

* See "The Spread of a Social Contagion" in this book.

Since the acting crowd is spontaneous, it knows no traditions or rules and has no official leaders. Acting, instead, on the basis of aroused impulses, it tends to be a nonmoral group. Its behavior may be irresponsible, even atrocious, vehement, violent, cruel, and destructive,* as in a mob scene. Lynching, beating, stoning, looting, dynamiting, and arson can result from this intense crowd-mindedness in which John Doe's usual critical ability seems to be suppressed.

The fourth type is the *expressive crowd*. In many ways it resembles the acting crowd, with this difference—no goal or objective emerges, and no plan of action develops. Yet tension has been built up.

What happens is that the tension becomes released in physical activity.† This may take the form of laughing, weeping, shouting, leaping, or dancing. The movement is often rhythmic, and typically it brings relief and joy to the members. It is sometimes seen in revival meetings, in the "holy dance" of certain religious sects, at rock concerts and at the "folk masses" of the "street people."

Exhilaration may be a part of a collective mood in which John Doe feels he is possessed or inspired by a supernatural spirit. When many persons share this feeling, it becomes accepted as a socially approved religious experience. At the height of ecstasy, the sublime feeling may be connected with persons or objects, and these may eventually become sacred. The appearance of sacred objects in this way may be the beginning of a cult or a primitive religion.

THE MASS

The breakup of small cultures, migration to the cities, mass communication, and education all join to create the new, wide world of *mass* man. The mass appears to contain many detached, uprooted, and sometimes alienated individuals who face fascinating, puzzling, even frightening new conditions of life. They act on their own, separately, as individuals rather than as members of

* See "Watts: Who Rioted and Why" in this book.
† See "The Flowering of the Hippie Movement" in this book.

groups. They do not interact as they would in a crowd; instead, each individual makes the same move or receives the same message, but without social interaction.* Examples are a mass migration (for example, the Klondike gold rush or the Oklahoma land boom) and the response to mass advertising in the media of mass communication—the movies, radio, TV, and the press.

In the mass, individual activities take the form of selections made according to individual needs: choices, for instance, of a new toothpaste, a party platform, a fashion, or a gospel. A new leader may emerge through mass communication and influence thousands of individuals to follow a new course.† The course may change existing political, economic, or religious organizations.

THE PUBLIC AND PUBLIC OPINION

The term *public* refers to a group of people (1) who are confronted by an issue, (2) who are divided in their ideas as to how to meet the issue, and (3) who engage in discussion over the issue. If there is no issue or no one discusses the issue—no one, for example, defends crime—there will be no public. Harry, Charlie, Estelle, and the others actually had formed a public after a few minutes of talk about pollution. They all agreed there was a problem but they had not come to a decision on how to combat the problem. The issue lay in their different opinions of ways and means.

The public differs markedly from the crowd. The crowd mills, develops a shared goal, and reaches unanimity. John Doe loses his individuality. On the other hand, the members of a public disagree with each other and argue but they—Harry, Charlie, Estelle, and the others—retain their individuality. Opposition, not agreement, marks the public.‡ Further, since argument must convince others, reason and logic are the mood of the public, rather than the emotion, rumor, and sentiment that dominate the crowd.

Public opinion, like the other forms of interaction just discussed, is a collective product. It is never unanimous, but is a

* See "Americans in a Time of Crisis" in this book.
† See "Black Nationalism" in this book.
‡ See "The Making of the President: 1940 and 1960" in this book.

composite reflecting the relative strength of the various single opinions of individuals. Once a decision is reached, public opinion recedes until the next issue appears; agreement brings public opinion to its end. Often it eventuates in a new law or changes in an old one. At other times it may result in a reconfirmation of existing legal forms.

Ordinarily, the public consists of two elements: interest groups and a more detached and spectator-like body of John Does. Interest groups stand to gain or lose from the issue. Thus trade unions, for example, can gain higher wages in an industrial dispute. The issue which creates the public is usually set by competing interest groups, each of which endeavors to win the support of the detached parties. The latter, as a result, are put in the position of judge. John Doe may ask questions of the interest groups and draw his own conclusions regarding the proposed solutions.

The detached, or, more exactly, the not-yet-attached are the very people whom interest groups and, particularly, lobbyists seek to win over to their side. Instead of using arguments, interest groups often employ *propaganda.** Propaganda is a deliberate campaign to induce people to accept a given view. Sentiment rather than reason is commonly invoked to win supporters who, like a public, will then act together on the basis of their convictions. In this respect propaganda differs from advertising, which woos people, one by one, to a certain line of action.

Any specific situation may contain portions of all three forms: the *crowd,* the *public,* and the *mass.* For example, when members of a public are aroused by propaganda appealing to sentiment, they begin to mill, crowd-like. In modern times, however, the public is more likely to be displaced by the mass. The increasing detachment of people from traditional life, the great number of public issues today, and the expansion of mass communication lead them increasingly to act on the basis of individual selection rather than on the basis of participation in public discussion. In many ways the public and the mass have become intermingled in modern times.

* See "War Toys and the Peace Movement" in this book.

SOCIAL MOVEMENTS

Social movements can be viewed as collective enterprises to establish, to a greater or lesser extent, a new order of life.* They arise from a feeling of widespread dissatisfaction. Gradually individuals express criticisms, wishes, and hopes, and prophets come to see a new vision of life. Interaction goes on as in a public and eventually a social movement may take form.

As a social movement develops, it comes to resemble a society. It acquires organization, leadership, and a division of labor, in short, a social structure. It also has a cultural structure: customs, traditions, rules, and values. Examples range from early Christianity to Communism, from the Prohibition Movement to the Civil Rights Movement.

Successful social movements go through four stages. First, the John Does, uneasy and restless, act in random fashion. But soon they grow aware that many others share their unrest. The second stage is that of popular excitement when goals come into focus. Then, in the stage of formalization, the movement becomes organized, with rules, policies, tactics, and discipline. When the final stage, institutionalization, is reached, the new organization sets out on the work of implementing the aims of the now-organized body. At each stage different types of leaders are required—agitators and prophets early in the cycle, statesmen and administrators later on.

During these stages, growth depends upon: agitation, the development of esprit de corps, morale, and an ideology.

Agitation. The function of agitation is to dislodge and liberate people for movement in new directions. In the early stages John Doe and others must be alerted to a specific injustice. Agitators and other spokesmen break down their old ways of thinking, jar them loose from traditional loyalties, and channel their feelings by means of criticism, prophesies and promises. Agitators help individuals to see themselves for the first time as persons with dignity, entitled to rights which they are being denied. Without this new self-conception (the "Black Power" theme of the late 1960s is a prime example), a movement lacks drive.

* See "Two Social Movements and Their Fates" in this book.

Agitators fall into two types. One is the biting critic, like Ralph Nader, whose taunts expose weaknesses in existing conditions. He goads his listeners to action. His function is to rouse consumers to a situation which they have long taken for granted and only now see "in its true light."

The second kind of agitator thrives where people are already made discontented by some grievance. He is like Hitler, able to infect others with his excitability.

The Development of Esprit de Corps. As the movement gathers strength, its members work and hope together, and criticize and encourage each other. Each sees in the other a comrade like himself in a great crusade. Together, they feel they have become new individuals with new aspirations and new identities. Thus many religious movements require converts to be "born again."

Esprit de corps develops in three ways: in the in-group-out-group relation, in the growth of informal fellowship, and in the development of ritual.* Blumer explains these three developments:

When "our" group regards another as an enemy, our feeling of *our* rightness, as against *their* villainy, reinforces our movement's solidarity.

Esprit de corps expands, also, in cooperative activities like singing, dancing, joking, and coining nicknames. Through such associations John Doe attains acceptance and status and the support of the group.†

Ritual and ceremonial behavior constitute the third means of developing esprit de corps. Mass meetings, rallies, parades, and demonstrations give the individual the feeling of personal enhancement. Slogans, songs, cheers, hymns, and uniforms heighten the feeling of the collective bond. Hitler's massed rallies with the brass bands, the goose-stepping regiments in perfectly disciplined line, and the massed red, white, and black banners 100 feet long were a classic crowd scene. They were also a brilliant example of the use of ceremony in heightening the commitment of the John Does of that time to the Nazi Movement.

---

* See "The Function of Ritual in an Organization" in *Social Organizations* in this *Readings in Sociology* Series.
† See "The Student Protesters" in this book.

Morale. But no social movement goes unchallenged by those who gain from the state of things as they are. What is needed to strengthen loyalties is morale. While esprit de corps gives enthusiasm and vigor to the movement, morale contributes persistency and determination. Morale passes the test if solidarity is preserved in the face of adversity.

Three kinds of belief contribute to morale: (1) evil and injustice will be banished and a perfect society will be attained; (2) the cause will win; (3) the movement's mission is sacred, that is, it is beyond question or criticism.

How is morale created? For one thing, all social movements have major and minor "saints," many of whom are endowed with miraculous powers and worshiped with reverence and awe. Examples of major saints are Hitler, Karl Marx, and Mary Baker Eddy. Instead of saints there may be heroes and martyrs, recent examples of whom are John F. Kennedy, Malcolm X, and Martin Luther King Jr.*

Two other aids to the building of morale are myths and sacred literature—Marx's *Das Kapital* and Hitler's *Mein Kampf* are the bibles of the Communist and the Nazi movements, respectively. The myths may proclaim the group as a chosen people. Or they may portray the inhumanity of the enemy, or depict the glorious brave new world which is certain to come if the faithful work devotedly toward it. Myths give a fixity to the beliefs of the followers and promote unquestioning acceptance of the leaders and the creeds.

Ideology. Along with morale, the ideology serves as a bulwark, especially when the movement is challenged. An ideology is a body of doctrine, beliefs, and myths. It gives to the movement justification, direction, weapons of attack and defense, inspiration, and hope. Much of the ideology is the best thought of the movement's intellectuals, and is aimed at gaining scholarly acceptance. At the same time the ideology has a popular side, designed to capture the John Does and expressed in slogans, folk arguments, stereotypes, and emotion-filled symbols.

There are many types of social movement. A *revolutionary* movement seeks to reconstruct the entire social order, not just to

* See "Hero Worship" in this book.

reform a portion of it. *Expressive* social movements take on the main features of the expressive crowd, and perpetuate them. This occurs often through the establishment of a religious cult with creed and set of rituals which change the moral lives of those who join. Movements in fashions rise in a changing society to express new tastes and dispositions, not only in clothing styles but in manners and the arts as well.* In *revivals* and *nationalistic* movements, people glorify the past, when, as they see it, "life was better."

This brief review only suggests the wide range of human behavior that falls outside of the group life regulated in organizations. In general, when John Doe is dissatisfied he becomes restless and ready to accept new ways. Eventually he finds others of the same mind. Out of this spontaneous milling interaction come, in the end, new organizations and, through them, social change.

* See "Fashion: The Rhythm of Change" in this book.

Whose Generation Gap?*

Do data from social surveys show that there is truth in the idea of a generation gap?

If there is evidence of a gap, can it be defined more precisely? Does it, for instance, concern certain categories of people and certain issues?

Is the generation gap the same thing among blacks as among whites?

Does the generation gap play a part in racial relationships?

The generation gap is a term referring to the differences in values and attitudes between young and old. The gap, a symptom of social change, is appearing all over the world. In the developing countries the young scandalize the old with their "modern" notions and "modern" ways (usually called "American" though they are found in all other industrialized, urbanized societies). When riots have closed some of India's universities for as long as two years; when in certain Latin American countries young radicals disrupt the legislatures and the courts; when in Japan students and police confront each other with sticks, clubs, and tear gas; and when there are demonstrations in the new cities of Africa, the young are expressing their violent disapproval of the way the old are "running the country." In these lands the traditions and the social worlds of young and old are more dramatically different than they are here. Yet the same symptoms of social change are painfully familiar, too, in Western Europe, Canada, and the United States of America.

It is convenient to think of the generation gap as caused by the fact that the wisdom of the elders no longer can help their children simply because of the years that separate them. But the idea has been analyzed

* Adapted from "What Generation Gap? A Comparison of Some Generational Differences Among Blacks and Whites" by Ann F. Brunswick, *Social Problems* (South Bend, Indiana: The Society for the Study of Social Problems), Vol. 17, No. 3 (Winter 1970), pp. 358–371. Reprinted by permission.

and refined. In the following selection, Ann F. Brunswick, social psychologist at Columbia University, reports research which interprets the generation gap as something more than a gap in age.

Mrs. Marshall could hardly believe her eyes when she turned to page three of her local paper. For there, staring her in the face, was a frightening picture of her son, under the headline:

Campus Afro Leader Threatens President with Student Boycott If Black Studies Program Not Implemented Immediately.

Mrs. Marshall could not understand why Jamey had become involved with this "nationalist" business. She had pleaded for months with him not to waste his energies on politics or other "useless" activities that wouldn't help him to get ahead in life. In her opinion, the NAACP was fine, but she thoroughly disapproved of her son's militant attitude toward civil rights and toward control in the black community.

Whenever she thought of the "unreasonable" demands he was making upon those in authority, she felt genuinely distressed. She and her husband had been serious students when they were in college; there had been just no place on campus for "agitators." Furthermore, had Mrs. Marshall not wanted Jamey to get his degree, she would almost have been glad to see him suspended—just to teach him a lesson. "Scolding gets a parent nowhere nowadays," she sighed to herself.

Cash Pulanski was just finishing his lunch when the peace demonstration started passing his construction site. There they were, he thought, every last "peacenik" and "freak" in town. As two wild-haired boys marched by, he yelled out: "Keep America beautiful. Cut your hair!" But the longer he watched, the less "funny" the kids seemed to him and the angrier he got. They wouldn't have been so smart-alecky, he felt, if they'd lived through the Depression, as he had. College students these days were just spoiled and lazy. They didn't appreciate America because they'd "had it too good." What's more, they looked like a cowardly bunch. He, for one, had been proud to serve in the army during World War II, but these "traitors" were waving signs accusing the United States of imperialism, war crimes—the whole works, in fact. Cash swore to himself: "If my kids grow up to be like this, I'll beat them to a pulp." Then the Viet Cong flag loomed into view. Before Cash realized what he was doing, he found himself pummeling the boy who was carrying it, trying to rip it out of his hands. Within seconds, all the hard-hats in the area had joined the fray, which soon turned into a full-scale riot.

Contests such as these between the young and their elders are an increasingly familiar feature of American life. Judging from the headlines, young people would appear to have little in common with their parents. That is not new. But they also differ from the rather conservative youth who reached maturity only ten or fifteen years before. But is it the changing times or the changing composition of the population that has catapulted the whole younger generation into such unprecedented prominence?

The young people who loom so large nowadays are, after all, only the "baby boom" children, grown up.* In 1970 there were 40 million Americans between the ages of 14 and 24. This was a 47 percent increase over the 1960 total. They constitute 20 percent of the total population, five percent more than their age category had reached in 1960. And their presence has made America a younger nation (the median age in 1970 was only 27.6 years) than it has been since 1930. But along with the greater leverage that relative numerical strength has brought them is a new phenomenon, usually referred to as the "generation gap." Yet, though many invoke the term to explain the often mystifying happenings in the world today, few seem able to agree on just what the expression means.

Some, like the psychiatrist Bruno Bettelheim, state that while the gap is real enough, it actually portends nothing new. Current youthful rebellions, he contends, are merely the latest manifestation of an age-old conflict between parents and children in which the young seek to "kill off" the old out of jealousy of their greater power and authority. Other observers, among them the anthro-

---

* See "The Baby Boom and How It Ended" in *Population Growth and the Complex Society* in this *Readings in Sociology* Series.

pologist Margaret Mead, argue that young people today are different because the world they live in is dramatically different from anything that existed before. In other words, they are responding to real problems in the objective world, not just to the inner stirrings of adolescence. Moreover, parents often do not consider as problems the things that perplex the young.*

Ann F. Brunswick believes that the generation gap is both real and unprecedented, but she demonstrates that it is not evenly distributed throughout society. For one thing, working-class youth and perhaps even the majority of white college students—at least those who have a definite career goal and a means of entering the occupational structure—do not differ widely from their parents in basic attitudes and values. Among these the generation gap is probably not particularly painful.

In contrast, two groups of youth—affluent white youth for whom survival no longer depends on the satisfaction of physical and material needs, and black youth who are seeking a new and equal role in American society—appear to be the principal actors in today's conflict between the generations. These groups are experiencing cultural discontinuity, that is, a gap between their world and their parents' world.

Dr. Brunswick, in order to pinpoint the differences between the generations in their basic attitudes toward life and society, singled out as topics for special attention: outlook on life, tolerance or hostility, and attitudes toward violence. She took her data from seven national surveys made between 1964 and 1969 among various segments of the population—black and white, young and old, college-educated and noncollege-educated. Thus she did not seek an explanation of the generation gap solely from young people, but inquired into the views of older people as well. This is what she found:

OUTLOOK ON LIFE

One nationwide survey (1969), designed to elicit information about the impact of changing socioeconomic conditions on

* See "Social Change and Parent-Youth Conflict" in *Life in Families* in this *Readings in Sociology* Series.

youth, had been made of a sample composed of 700 college whites, 50 college blacks, 600 noncollege whites, 84 noncollege blacks, and 700 parents, undifferentiated by race or education (Table 1). Asked to say who was more optimistic about the future—parent or child—roughly half the youth in all four categories considered themselves more optimistic than their parents; only about a fifth of the young people considered their parents more optimistic. The older generation apparently underrated the optimism of youth; only 38 percent of them rated their children more optimistic than they (the parents) were. On this point, educational and racial differences proved of no consequence. On the whole, each generation thought the other was more pessimistic.

Parents as a group tended to brush off the differences between their own and their children's values (Table 1, second question). Half the parents, for instance, considered the difference in generational values "very slight," whereas only a third of the young people (30 percent of white college youth and 38 percent of white noncollege youth) saw the situation in this happy light. Between 14 and 29 percent of the youth thought the difference "very great," while only nine percent of the parents believed it to be so serious. It was black youth who had not gone to college who were convinced of the greatest differences in values between the generations. White youth, regardless of their education, were less conscious of a generation gap.

These findings seemed to contradict the common idea of the generation gap, for the two generations on the whole agreed on the size of the gap (Table 1, third question). Roughly seven in ten in both groups thought that it existed but was exaggerated. However, Dr. Brunswick thinks the seeming contradiction could be due to the way the questions were worded—a persistent difficulty in surveys. Once again, black noncollege youth (37 percent) were in the forefront of those who spoke of a "yawning" gap. Very few in any group said there was no generation gap at all.

A substantial number of college youth consider themselves to be outside the mainstream of American thinking. This fact came to light when young people were asked whether they thought their own views were shared by most Americans. Of youth in college, only a third of the white and a quarter of the black felt the majority of Americans shared their beliefs. But over

24

half the young people not in college, black and white, estimated that their ideas matched those of the majority of Americans (Table 1, fourth question). In contrast, a full 67 percent of the parents thought their views were in line with what most Americans believed. These findings suggest that it is the college youth of both races who feel most alienated from their fellow citizens, while parents in general are more in agreement with their fellow citizens.

Finally, both generations were asked their opinions on how much an individual can control his own life (Table 1, fifth question). Over three-fourths of the noncollege youth together with nearly as great a proportion of the parents (77, 79, and 74 percent) declared that they believed an individual's destiny lies largely in his own hands. Here there is no generation gap at all. But in contrast, only between 61 and 62 percent of the college-educated youth shared this view. Indeed, the college students, who in reality have a larger number of options in life and a superior chance of succeeding in the occupations they choose, were more pessimistic than were those whose lives have been determined to a much greater degree by outside forces. This belief in their own powerlessness possibly contributes to the alienation and frustration of college-bred youth.

In summary: On two of the five questions on outlook on life (Table 1), less educated youth, in general, were likely to approach closest to the views of their parents. But this does not seriously challenge the notion of the generation gap, for young people of both races and both educational categories differ from their parents on the other topics: optimism, the size of the gap, and the sense of belonging in the mainstream of American life. At this point, then, research has established one important fact, namely, that the generation gap is not a wholesale affair. It seems to be wide in some areas of life, between some kinds of parents and offspring, and narrower in others.

Turning to a survey made a year earlier (in 1968), Dr. Brunswick noted that older blacks were more aware of the improvements in the condition of Negro Americans than were younger blacks. But among young blacks between the ages of 20 and 39, the better educated were more aware of racial progress than were the less educated. On this point, then, the generation gap

TABLE 1 *
Attitudes Toward Life of Parents and of Black and White Youth

	PARENTS	COLLEGE YOUTH		NONCOLLEGE YOUTH	
		WHITE	BLACK	WHITE	BLACK
TOTAL NUMBER	700	673	50	532	84
Who Is More Optimistic About the Future?					
Child	38%	48%	57%	52%	53%
Parent	25	19	18	19	25
Same, D.K.† N.A.‡	37	33	25	29	22
How Great Is the Difference Between the Parent's and Child's Values?					
Very Great	9%	15%	18%	14%	29%
Moderate	40	55	53	48	44
Very Slight	51	30§	29	38	27§
How Great Is the Generation Gap?					
Large	22%	24%	29%	27%	37%
Exists, But Exaggerated	70	73	69	67	50

None	6	2	2	4	13
D.K.† N.A.‡	2	1	—	2	—

Do You Think Your Own Views Are Shared by Most Americans?

Yes	67%	34%	24%	53%	54%
Not Sure	20	29	45	28	31
No	13	37	31	19	15

Depending on How Much Strength and Character a Person Has, Can He Pretty Well Control What Happens to Him?

Believe	74%	62%	61%	77%	79%
Do Not Believe	24	38	39	23	21
D.K.† N.A.‡	2	—	—	—	—

* Data from Daniel Yankelovich: Youth and Parent Survey, 1969 (unpublished).
† Don't Know.
‡ No Answer.
§ Includes D.K./N.A., one, and two percent respectively.

among black Americans was greatest between the less educated and their elders.

On a related question—whether blacks could get ahead in spite of prejudice and discrimination—the least hopeful were the teenagers and those under 40 years of age who had not completed high school. But responses to this question and the one before it may simply be a realistic appraisal by young, uneducated blacks of their poor prospects in life, as compared with the brighter futures they could expect today if they had had more education. In the minds of the young, the progress noted by the older generation on all levels may be exclusively enjoyed by the more fortunate levels of black society, not by blacks as a whole.

INTERRACIAL TOLERANCE AND HOSTILITY

The relations between white and black Americans are a vital and sensitive area of national life, and there the generation gap appears again. Dr. Brunswick refers to a 20-year study (1942–1963) of the attitudes of white respondents toward blacks which brought to light a direct relationship between age and pro-integration sentiment. In other words, the younger an individual, the more he favored integration. This is a simple case of the gap between the generations. However, education divided the survey even more dramatically. The difference between the least educated (who were least in favor of racial integration) and the best educated (most approved of integration) was even greater than the difference between the oldest and youngest age groups. In sum, younger and better educated whites were more tolerant racially and more pro-integrationist in outlook than were older whites with less education. Depending on their schooling, the gap would be wide in some white families and narrow in others.

In contrast, Negro attitudes toward whites present a more complicated picture. The National Advisory Commission on Civil Disorders commissioned an opinion poll in 1968 of a sample of 2600 whites and 2800 blacks. The poll yielded a picture of generational differences among blacks that is almost the reverse of that prevailing among whites. In other words, younger blacks as a whole appeared more hostile to whites (or to have worse impressions of them) than did older blacks (Table 2). As among the

TABLE 2 *
Attitudes of Blacks Toward White People

EDUCATION		8TH GRADE OR LESS			12TH GRADE		COMPLETE COLLEGE	
NUMBER OF WHITES WHO DISLIKE NEGROES:	Age:	16–19	20–39	40–69	20–39	40–69	20–39	40–69
	Number:	(362)	(113)	(490)	(498)	(221)	(59)	(35)
Few		38%	28%	39%	33%	38%	38%	60%
Many		47	42	40	51	47	53	34
Almost All		12	22	11	12	8	6	5
Don't Know		3	8	10	4	7	3	1
Do Most Whites Want a Better Break for Negroes?		27%	18%	31%	28%	39%	17%	46%
Do Most Whites Want to Keep the Negro Down?		29	32	26	29	24	16	15
Do Most Whites Not Care?		40	38	27	36	30	64	29
Don't Know		4	12	16	7	7	3	10

* Adapted from "Racial Attitudes in Fifteen American Cities" by Angus Campbell and Howard Shuman, *The National Advisory Commission on Civil Disorder* by The Koerner Commission—(Washington, D.C.: United States Government Printing Office, June 1968).

whites, there is an age gap but the generations have changed sides.

Education, again, modified attitudes. Those with the greatest misgivings about whites were blacks between the ages of 20 and 39 who had had only a grammar school education: Twenty-two percent of them believed that "almost all whites dislike Negroes." This contrasts with only one-half that number in the 4- to 69-year-old category with similar education and with one-fourth of that number among 40 to 69-year-olds with a college education. Similarly, more than any other group, the young and least educated blacks believed that "most whites want to keep the Negro down." The least hostile to whites were the older (ages 40 to 69) college-educated blacks.

In every educational category, blacks under 40 consistently had more unfavorable views of the intentions of white people than did blacks who were over 40. While college education tended to moderate unfavorable impressions of whites among blacks under 40, it still did not bring them to think of whites as friendly and sympathetic.

The sharpest split between the black generations appeared within the college-educated group. For instance, 53 percent of the younger college graduates believed that many whites disliked blacks as compared with only 34 percent of the older graduates. Similarly, only 17 percent of the younger college blacks believed that most whites wanted "a better break" for the black, as opposed to a more optimistic 46 percent of the older generation. Thus among the well educated the picture is repeated: the old differ from the young, and the old are more tolerant.

Several surveys studied by Ann Brunswick dealt with separatist (as opposed to integrationist) sentiment among black Americans. This kind of thinking was especially common among teenagers and those in their twenties.

One form of separatist sentiment is a belief in self-determination—for example: "Stores in black neighborhoods should be owned and run by blacks"; "A school with mostly black children should have mostly black teachers." This attitude drew the greatest support among young (20 to 39 years old) black college graduates—30 percent and 20 percent, respectively, agreed to these two statements. Plainly, integration as a broad goal still retains its appeal for most black Americans. Among them education softens antiwhite hostility but also increases support for self-determination.*

To summarize: Unlike the intolerance of old age in the white population, interracial sympathy among blacks is greatest in the older people, especially the better educated. It is least prevalent in the young blacks, particularly the least educated. Thus, while young whites show increasing interracial sympathy, young blacks seem to be growing more and more alienated and hostile. Education is crucial in the attitudes of both races but seems more likely to produce a wary cynicism on the part of young college blacks today than the tolerance it inspires in young whites.

ATTITUDES TOWARD VIOLENCE

Not surprisingly, a definite generational difference was found in connection with attitudes toward violence. Younger people of either race were more inclined to advocate or to accept violent means of protest than were their elders. The young people in black families, according to the survey, were readier to use violence than were the young in white families. And among youths of both races, the college-educated were more favorable to violent methods than were the less well educated. The generation gap was, one supposes, least apparent in families, black or white, where schooling had been scanty.

On the subject of rioting a true generational gap appeared. Asked how they viewed recent ghetto disturbances—whether mainly as protest, mainly as looting, or as a little of both—the respondents between the ages of 20 and 39, both black and white and in almost every educational category, were more disposed to see the riots as social protest than were respondents between the ages of 40 and 69. The latter condemned rioting as law-breaking. But the generation gap was greatest between young black college graduates and older black college graduates: Sixty-one percent of those between the ages of 20 and 39 interpreted the riots chiefly

* See "Who Is Against Desegregation?" in *Racial and Ethnic Relations* in this *Readings in Sociology* Series.

as protest in contrast to only 33 percent of those between the ages of 40 and 69. Riots could be a painful subject in the families of educated blacks, where the range of attitude is so great.

On the question whether the riots helped or hurt the cause of black Americans, the gap between the generations among blacks was even more striking: The highest proportion approving riots was among black college youth and the lowest was among older college-educated blacks. The split in attitudes between the generations in black families was very large; in fact two and one-half times larger than in white families.

CONCLUSION

As can be seen from these surveys of basic attitudes, the generation gap is a far more complex phenomenon than is frequently supposed. One thing is certain: Age is not the only force widening the chasm between the various sectors of society. For another, there is not simply one generation gap. There appear to be several, each one wide or narrow in response to particular social pressures and dependent upon what elements in the population are involved. Education is at least as important as age as a determiner of "generations."

Yet the generation gap cannot simply be shrugged off as an education gap, for young and old who are on the same educational level continue to be separated. Young blacks who are college graduates, in fact, appear to be further apart from the college graduates among their elders than are the young from the old in any other category in either race—evidence of the number and variety of generation gaps that have surfaced in the various segments of society.

For much of society, the generation gap is not great. Working-class youth see the world, on the whole, much as their parents see it. And white youth with a college education and a fair certainty of attaining the careers they hope to enter share their elders' basic values. But for the rest of society the gap is a yawning one. Two groups of young people have emerged as the principal activators of the generation gap. One is the minority of white college youth—the minority that enrages the Cash Pulanskis in the country—who feel they need a new set of values, attitudes, and standards with which to find their way into society.* The other group is black youth in general, spearheaded by the college intellectuals but containing an increasingly militant ghetto population as well. The latter group, from a quite different standpoint, feel the same need for radical change in American society. Jamey Marshall is one of them. He and his fellow rebels seem to be leaving the "older" generation—whether they be old or young in years, educated or uneducated—far behind.

Dr. Brunswick concludes that it is unlikely that the two groups will abandon their youthful behavior and attitudes upon reaching the magic age of 30. Rather, their responses to the world around them might more accurately be interpreted as early signs of more general trends of the future. It is after all the young who notify the old whether life is represented by the older generation has meaning. And it is the young who have the power to carry on society as it is, to reform it, or to rebel against it.

* See "The Student Protesters" and "The Flowering of the Hippie Movement" in this book.

Americans in a Time of Crisis*

How does the American public receive word of extraordinary news events?

In what different ways do people react personally to such an event as the killing of a President?

Does the assassination of a President unify or divide the American public?

What is the effect of a Presidential assassination on basic American values?

Bob Wingate had been doing errands during his lunch hour and was walking back to the office. Passing a garage he noticed a group of auto mechanics and attendants with their heads together, all looking as if they were straining to hear something. As Bob hurried by, he heard one man say: "I can't believe it!"

Thirty seconds after Bob had reached his desk, Murray from the next office appeared at his door, saying: "My wife just called me. Did you hear the news?" Then, after explaining briefly, Murray went into the boss's office and brought back a transistor radio. Together they listened, joined first by one and then eventually by all of their grim-faced colleagues. No one did any more work that afternoon.

Jack Ferrero had been driving along the open highway, en route to a midafternoon sales meeting. Turning off into the small town which was his destination, he noticed that the streets looked even quieter than usual. Not a single person for seven whole

* Adapted from "The Assassination of President Kennedy: A Preliminary Report on Public Reactions and Behavior" by Paul B. Sheatsley and Jacob J. Feldman, *Public Opinion Quarterly*, Vol. 28, No. 2 (Summer 1964), pp. 189–215. Reprinted by permission.

blocks! Even the familiar "round the clock" delicatessen where he usually stopped for cigarettes was shut, with no sign explaining why. Where was everyone?

Still puzzled, Jack entered the main door of the building to go to his sales meeting—only to be informed by an elderly janitor that the building was closed and that everyone had gone home. Jack just had time to thunder, "What's going on around this place?" before he noticed that the janitor was weeping silently. He then learned what almost everyone else in America had already known for close to three hours—that President John F. Kennedy was dead, assassinated in Dallas earlier that day, November 22, 1963.

Few who lived through that event—and the intense three and a half days that followed—will ever forget it. Ordinary life came to a complete halt. Trading on the New York Stock Exchange ceased at 2:07 P.M. that day—just an hour after the President died—and was not resumed until the subsequent Tuesday. Government and business offices dismissed their staff, theaters and restaurants shut down, and millions of small shops across the country quietly closed their doors between November 22 and November 25.

Over the weekend there was increasingly heavy attendance at worship services conducted in honor of the fallen President— all leading up to the state funeral on November 25, which the new chief executive had declared to be a day of national mourning. Throughout the period, traffic in many cities was reduced to a trickle, and on Monday, the 25th, even the railroads halted for a two-minute tribute. The whole world seemed to have disappeared indoors.

In short, people put aside their usual concerns and obligations to give their undivided attention to details of the tragic happening. And inasmuch as all TV and radio stations had cancelled whatever commercials and entertainment programs they had previously scheduled in order to devote full network time to news about the assassination, more people were caught up in the unfolding drama than had ever before been gripped by a political event.

Other Presidents—among them Lincoln, Garfield, and McKinley—had been murdered in office. But their deaths had occurred more than 60 years before and few citizens in 1963 were old enough to remember that far back. The sudden death, in 1945, of President Roosevelt, then an elderly man, had occurred within the lifetimes of a large segment of the population. But this time it was the cutting off in the prime of life of a youthful, vigorous, first-term leader who was also the father of two small children. In short, the event itself was different. The whole nation gave it the closest attention, responding all at the same time to the same news.

But while the nation abandoned normal routines and focused its attention entirely on the assassination and the funeral, the sociologists plunged into research. Some 25 studies were undertaken immediately. One of these was the work of the National Opinion Research Center (NORC), an organization at the University of Chicago set up to discover and analyze public opinion. On Sunday, November 24, the day before the President's funeral, the NORC decided upon a national survey, with Paul B. Sheatsley and Dr. Jacob J. Feldman in charge of research. Three days later the NORC's staff of local interviewers, stationed at various locations across the country, started on their assignments. Through very hard work, the interviewing was completed by Saturday, November 30.

HOW THE NEWS SPREAD

One of the most interesting facts learned from the NORC's survey was how quickly the mass media and word of mouth can spread the news of a major event. President Kennedy was shot at 12:30 P.M. (Central Standard Time) on Friday and was pronounced dead a half hour later at 1:00 P.M. By that time 68 percent, or two out of every three adult Americans, had heard the news. Within another hour, an additional 24 percent learned of the assassination. Thus, in less than two hours, 92 percent of the public was aware of the event. By 6:00 P.M. word had reached 99.8 percent of the American people. This abnormally fast and broad diffusion of the news was probably without parallel in human history.

About half the people (47 percent) received word of the assassination by means of radio and television, the other half (49 percent) through telephone calls or personal messages. Only four percent first learned of the tragedy from newspapers or other sources. Half the adult population were at home when they first got the news; 29 percent were at work; and 21 percent were outside, shopping, having lunch, driving, or occupied elsewhere away from home. Only one-third were alone when they received the news. All these circumstances—the time of day when the event took place, where people were at the moment, and who was with them—were factors that had some effect on how people were likely to react.

FIRST REACTIONS

What did people feel and how did they behave immediately after getting the news?

The majority (54 percent) of the public said they did not continue their usual activities after they heard of the assassination. Of those who did continue with what they were doing, most said they found it difficult to go on. Only 19 percent reported that they were able to carry on "pretty much as usual." Of those who dropped what they were doing, five out of six turned to television or radio immediately. Most of the others hurried home to tune in or phoned or visited friends to talk about the news.

Fifty-four percent of the public said they "felt like talking about it with other people." However, another 40 percent "felt more like being by myself." Apparently, the more people admired the late President, the more likely they were to want to be alone after they heard of his death. For example, 51 percent of the blacks, as contrasted with only 28 percent of southern whites who had opposed Kennedy in 1960, said they felt "more like being by themselves."

The majority of all respondents could not recall any other time in their lives when they had had the sort of feeling they experienced when they heard of President Kennedy's assassination. Most of the 47 percent who could think of such an occasion referred to the death of a parent or other relative, or a close friend. Blacks and pro-Kennedy northerners were much more likely to fall into this category; in fact, 80 percent of the blacks referred to an occasion of personal grief. Southerners and anti-Kennedy northerners, on the other hand, referred more often to the death of Roosevelt or to Pearl Harbor.

The respondents were questioned as to the sort of person who committed the crime. Four-fifths of the people interviewed thought they knew immediately upon learning of the shooting what the criminal was like. Almost half thought the act was the work of a crazed or fanatical individual ("insane," "mentally unbalanced," "a nut," or "an extremist"). Many gave the assassin credit for a political motive or a motive growing out of some system of ideas—that is, for ideological reasons.

For instance: About a quarter of the population immediately suspected a Communist, Castro-ite, or other leftist. An eighth thought the shots were probably fired by a segregationist or other representative of the right wing. In fact, of the one-third of all blacks who suspected there was an ideological motive behind the assassination, two out of three blamed a segregationist. By contrast, whites, whether northern or southern, pro- or anti-Kennedy, were much more likely to attribute the deed to a Communist or a supporter of Castro.

Pity, loss, sorrow, shame, and anger dominated the citizens' feelings. In fact, from 73 to 92 percent of all people shared in one or another of these five reactions—those who had opposed the President reported them in only slightly less degree than those who had been his supporters. Thus, the commonest immediate response was to see the drama primarily in human terms, as both a personal and national tragedy.

Nevertheless, a substantial minority was concerned with the political, international, economic, and moral implications of the event. Forty-seven percent immediately worried about the effect of the assassination on the "political situation" in the country. The fact that this was mentioned by almost two-thirds of the blacks and also by a solid majority of southern white supporters of Kennedy suggests that they were thinking of the fate of the civil rights program. The intensity of black reaction to the event is also shown by the fact that two-thirds of them, as compared with only 38 percent of the general public, were "so confused and upset, they didn't know what to feel." Again, a full half of the black population, compared with only 20 percent of the general public was "worried how this might affect my own life, job, and future."

THE FOUR DAYS

The four days following the President's assassination were an abnormal period during which most Americans were spellbound, totally absorbed in the high drama unfolding before them. The average adult spent eight hours on Friday, ten hours on Saturday, eight hours on Sunday, and ten hours on Monday, the day of the funeral, watching television or listening to the radio. Overwhelmed by the details of first one and then of a second murder (that of Oswald), which the mass media presented to them, not surprisingly many in this vast audience began to suffer from physical and psychological symptoms.

How did people respond after the first shock and disbelief had turned to a deepening sense of loss, sadness, shame, and despair? From the answers the sociologists received, it would appear that the process of mass mourning, though telescoped in time, has much in common with the stages individuals go through when they have lost someone close to them (See the Table).

For example, two out of three respondents reported that they "felt very nervous and tense" during this period. Fifty-seven percent said that they "felt sort of dazed and numb." A majority confessed that there were times during the four days when they cried. Almost half the public found it hard to get to sleep, and over 40 percent said they "felt more tired than usual" or "didn't feel like eating." Still others (34 percent) "kept forgetting things." Again, blacks and Kennedy supporters were more likely to experience these symptoms and to feel them more severely than were persons politically opposed to the late President. However, few in any category were entirely free of bodily symptoms of reaction.

Yet, as with reactions to more personal grief, the physical symptoms were relatively short lived. By the time of the interview, two to five days later, fewer than one person in four reported any bodily symptoms and fully half the population felt none of them. But here again, black citizens and white Kennedy supporters suffered from abnormal symptoms for a longer period than others did.

In ascertaining the feelings of children, the sociologists thought that teenagers would react just as the adults did and that children under four would not be affected at all. One-third of

TABLE

Immediate Reactions to the News of the Assassination

Symptoms During the Four Days	National Sample	Total Black	White Pro-K * North	White Pro-K South	White Non-K † North	White Non-K South
Didn't feel like eating	43%	58%	52%	38%	31%	26%
Smoked much more than usual	29	40	33	34	19	21
Had headaches	25	43	28	24	17	12
Had an upset stomach	22	26	28	17	14	14
Cried	53	62	61	53	42	34
Had trouble getting to sleep	48	68	50	53	36	39
Felt very nervous and tense	68	80	72	69	57	56
Felt like getting drunk	4	11	4	1	3	1
Felt more tired than usual	42	61	43	46	32	34
Felt dizzy at times	12	30	12	12	6	5
Lost temper more than usual	19	28	23	13	13	10
Hands sweat and felt damp and clammy	17	26	19	20	8	10
Had rapid heart beat	26	44	30	28	13	16
Felt "sort of" dazed and numb	57	57	65	64	46	47
Kept forgetting things	34	56	39	35	19	22
Felt none of these	11	4	8	11	18	18
Number of cases	(1,384)	(165)	(568)	(184)	(329)	(138)

* pro-K means pro-Kennedy
† non-K means not pro-Kennedy

the surveyed families included one or more children between the ages of four and twelve. The research teams asked their parents to tell how the children received the news. It turned out that

CROWD AND MASS BEHAVIOR

23 percent were "very upset," 45 percent were "somewhat upset," and 30 percent were "not upset at all" (two percent gave no answer). These are lower than the figures on adult reactions. Thus it must be concluded that the children were less distressed than the grownups.

ATTITUDES TOWARD THE ASSASSINATION

The primary purpose of the National Opinion Research Center's survey was to find out what the people did and felt in the wake of a sudden national emergency. The sociologists designed further questions to probe the public's attitudes toward the alleged assassin, Lee Harvey Oswald. They also wanted to know the public's idea of Jack Ruby, who killed Oswald, and of the "basic causes," if any, of the tragic events. The answers to these questions tell something about the political climate of the United States in the early 1960s.

As can be seen from the responses to the open-ended question, "Who or what should really be blamed for the assassination of President Kennedy—aside from the man who actually fired the gun?" there was no general agreement concerning the final responsibility. For instance, 41 percent either had no opinion or blamed only the assassin, while about 25 percent placed the blame on the public generally. Some blamed the environment, using phrases like the "prevailing climate of hatred," "social tensions," "the decline of morals." Still another 14 percent specifically blamed the assassination on inadequate measures to protect the President.

Only one person in five answered in ideological terms. Fifteen percent blamed Communists or leftists; five percent blamed right-wingers or segregationists. All the others, that is, four-fifths of the population, declined to see the assassination as a political crime, but instead declared it to be an isolated example of abnormal behavior.

At the time of the interview, 72 percent were "pretty much convinced" that Lee Harvey Oswald was the assassin. However, there was no agreement on why the assassin, whoever he was, had done the deed. A third attributed the action to mental illness, 16 percent blamed Communism or left-wing sympathies, and three percent blamed right-wing sympathies. Twelve percent thought the assassin had a grudge against the President or the government, and another 12 percent thought he hated everybody or was generally disgruntled and unhappy.

Interestingly, 23 percent of the public thought either that the assassin had been paid to do the job or that he had been ordered or persuaded to do it by some unspecified group. Over twice that number (62 percent) suspected that "other people were involved," in other words, that there had been a conspiracy. Only 24 percent felt the assassination was the work of one man alone.

Public reaction both to the alleged assassin of the President and to the killer of Oswald himself provided the sociologists with evidence that the great majority of the people continued to have faith in the traditions of justice and fair play. Even after Ruby shot Oswald before a TV audience of 60 million, fewer than one in five of those interviewed expressed satisfaction. About one-third were sorry that Oswald had been deprived of due process of law and a fair trial, while another third regretted that his death made it impossible ever to learn the truth. Thus, in spite of the unsettling effects of these two shocking events, probably two-thirds of the population stood firm in their respect for legal processes and their faith that justice could or would be done.

One of the principal political effects of the assassination was to raise the late President instantly in the estimation of his countrymen. Asked to rate Kennedy, a full half of the adult population—in the days immediately following the tragedy—called him "one of the two or three best Presidents the country ever had." An additional 28 percent described him as "better than average," while only two percent termed him "somewhat below average" or "one of the worst Presidents the country ever had." However, when 78 percent of the nation gave him such high marks, it was in sharp contrast to their rating of him on the Gallup Poll just two weeks before his death. At that time, only 59 percent of the population approved of "the way Kennedy was handling his job as President," while 28 percent disapproved and 13 percent were undecided. Grief, pity, sentiment, fear of the unknown, plus a temporary suspension of critical judgment obviously did much to enhance the nation's estimate of its Chief Executive.

CONCLUSIONS

What, then, did the sociologists conclude from the national survey? This is how they summarized their basic findings:

The increasing size and urbanization of the population, together with the prevalence of radio and television, now make it possible for virtually 100 percent of the public to become aware of a crucial event within a few hours. Efficient modern communication introduces a new element in historical events.

The assassination of the President engaged the deep emotions of practically everyone. Events of this order—which produce a stoppage of ordinary activities, an almost complete preoccupation with the event, and actual physical symptoms all across the nation—are extremely rare.

Despite the bitterness of everyday partisan debate, the great majority of the people come to the support even of political opponents in times of national crisis. Few people excuse violence as a political weapon.

There was a strong tendency to see the assassination in personal rather than political terms. Thus, the reactions of the public followed a pattern of grief that is typical of those who have suddenly suffered some close personal bereavement.

Almost universal mourning followed the President's death and at once he became a heroic figure. This is not quite such an extraordinary happening as most people believed at the time. It has occurred before under similar circumstances.

The response of the public to the shooting was not ideological—that is, only a minority blamed the assassination on either Communists or right-wingers. Most people felt the lesson to be learned was of the evil consequences of hatred and intolerance.

Neither the public's sense of justice nor its belief in the judicial system was fundamentally shaken by the two shocking acts of violence which occurred over the weekend of November 22.

The majority believed that the assassin did not act alone although this was inconsistent with the tone of the findings as a whole. However, it suggests that many people do not accept mental illness as an explanation of behavior. To them a conspiracy is more comprehensible and less threatening than the idea of wild, random behavior as an explanation of extraordinary events.

Finally, did the assassination of President Kennedy change the American people in any fundamental way? The strange thing, the sociologists found, was that in spite of the vivid impression it made on all citizens, the event had practically no effect—even in the short run—on the basic beliefs and values of the nation. As later opinion polls showed, the assassination did not make Americans more or less anti-Communist. It did not change their attitudes toward civil rights. It did not alter their basic optimism about other people's motives. And it did not make them any more or less religious. It shook them temporarily—that is all.

How New Ideas Spread*

How do new ideas spread?

Can the mass media "brainwash" people into trying something new?

Rumors, fashions, and technological changes diffuse quickly in modern society. Is this because the mass media have replaced conversation as the major form of communication?

Just before planting season, Kenny Walker, owner of Walker's Feed and Grain Store in Newfane, Iowa, told his customers about a new type of hybrid corn seed developed by scientists at the state university.

"Supposed to triple the crop of corn per acre," claimed Kenny.

Most farmers were skeptical. The farming traditions were strong in Iowa. Few men dared change the old ways.

"The county extension agent says this seed has been tested and proved good," urged Kenny. "Don't cost much more than the regular seed, either."

The Newfane farmers still thought they'd rather not try it. That county agricultural agent always had some crazy, new-fangled ideas, anyhow, they said.

But Al Henchell, a young man who had just taken over his father's farm after spending a year at the state university, decided he might test out a little of the seed.

"What the heck, Kenny! I can't lose anything," he said. "Besides, those professors usually know what they're talking about. I'll plant a few acres and see how it compares with the regular seed."

---

* Adapted from "The Social Itinerary of Technical Change: Two Studies on the Diffusion of Innovation" by Elihu Katz. Reproduced by the permission of the Society for Applied Anthropology from *Human Organization*, Vol. 20, No. 2, 1961, pp. 70–80.

At harvest time that year, farmers who dropped by Al's place found him enthusiastic over the results of his experiment. More important, they could see the proof—larger ears of corn with more even, more pulpy, rows of big yellow kernels.

The next year other young farmers decided to follow Al's example, and Kenny Walker stocked a little more of the hybrid seed. During the following winter, whenever farmers gathered at social events or Grange meetings, the experimenters talked about their improved crop. By the third spring, almost half of the local farmers bought and planted some of the new seed.

Within the next six or seven years, nearly everyone had at least tried the hybrid corn. Many farmers even planted it exclusively. In fact, Kenny Walker found he was now stocking more hybrid seed than regular.

The new idea was not "new" anymore. It had become accepted in the Iowa Corn Belt.

How can you describe the process that carries a new idea or innovation from its conception in a laboratory or a lecture hall to its adoption and use by the general public? Or a new product from the manufacturer to the customer?

This process, the diffusion of innovation, is of great interest to social scientists for it is the mechanism by which new forms of culture and of behavior are developed and transmitted to the societies of the future. Some innovations are made by organized effort—the newspaper plant is highly organized editorially and mechanically to prepare and sell a commodity, the news. But news, as everyone knows, has other ways of spreading, notably in the unorganized mode of transmission from person to person.* Unorganized, unstructured dissemination of a new thing is the subject that interests Elihu Katz, professor of sociology at the University of Chicago and at the Hebrew University of Jerusalem. He has analyzed the diffusion of innovations in his own studies and he has assembled the facts about contrasting situations from research done by others.

In the 1950s, two sociologists, Neal Gross and Bryce Ryan, studied how the hybrid corn gained acceptance among the farm-

---

* See "Americans in a Time of Crisis" in this book.

ers in two Iowa communities. Their findings were compared by Katz with the findings he arrived at in work with James Coleman and Herbert Menzel. The research of these three sociologists showed how doctors in four midwestern communities responded to the appearance on the market of a new "miracle drug."

The two studies reached surprisingly similar conclusions. And, simply because corn and drugs and farmers and doctors are so radically different the findings indicate that the diffusion of innovation may work in very much the same way in all sorts of situations.

THE RESEARCH DESIGN

The two research programs were very much alike. Both were concerned with a "campaign," that is, an attempt to change attitudes, opinions, or actions.

All campaigns have the same basic elements: a new idea or product is introduced over a period of time through various channels of communication within a social structure. Professor Katz began with the belief that the design of the two research studies—drugs and corn—can best be seen in terms of these four basic elements.

A New Product

Hybrid corn was first made available in 1927 and was almost universally accepted within ten years. Gammanym, just one of many "miracle drugs" introduced in the early 1950s for treating infections, was accepted almost everywhere in the United States within less than two years.

The two products have many similarities not easily seen at first. Each came highly recommended by respected scientific authorities. Each was of central importance to the men who used it. Each produced noticeable results that allowed users to see for themselves that it was an improvement over old means.

Both the corn and the gammanym could be adopted in installments. A farmer, for example, might experiment by planting only a few acres of the new seed one year and checking them against his regular crop. The doctors could give gammanym to a few patients and check their recovery rate against patients who were kept on more conventional drugs. Obviously, this is different from such all-or-nothing innovations as a new car. You cannot buy half a Mustang one year, and then pick up the rest later if you like it.

Both of the innovations were really only modifications of products already existing. As a result, adopting the new seed or drug required only minor—although still significant—changes in old patterns of thought and action. By contrast, campaigns for birth control or sanitation in underdeveloped nations often are hampered by powerful traditions, beliefs, and superstitions.*

THE TIME FACTOR

In both studies, the new product was considered accepted by the very first use of any amount of it, no matter how small the amount. Thus, in each study the research team was able to assign a date to the initial use of the new product and to chart the rate of acceptance by various other individuals.

CHANNELS OF COMMUNICATION

The research workers asked all the farmers and the doctors how they had first heard of the new products. From the answers, the sociologists attempted to reconstruct patterns of the first news, any later and reinforcing information, and the final arguments which won over even those who were slowest to be convinced.

Among the impersonal channels mentioned by the doctors and farmers were journals, direct mail advertisements, and radio and newspaper stories. Among the personal channels were salesmen, colleagues, and friends.

SOCIAL STRUCTURES

Social structures, such as the Grange among the farmers or the local medical association among the doctors, provide the boundaries within which an innovation may spread. Inside each of these social structures, individual members occupy various ranks, so it is possible to find how those of different status react

* See "Folklore and the Birth Rate: The Case of Japan" in *Population Growth and the Complex Society* in this *Readings in Sociology* Series.

CROWD AND MASS BEHAVIOR

to new ideas. Moreover, the social structure also provides a network of communication which allows the sociologist to trace the path of a new idea.

For this purpose, in addition to the standard questions about age, education, and interests, the doctors were asked to name: their three best friends who were doctors, the three or four physicians to whom they turned for consultation, and the colleagues whom they most often asked for advice on the use of drugs. By this means, the doctors could be located in the social structure in terms of friendships, case discussions, and advice. Each doctor could also be rated according to his integration in the profession, that is, his popularity (how many other doctors he named as friends, consultants, or colleagues) and his status (which doctors named him).

The research workers who analyzed the diffusion of hybrid corn did not go into such detail. But they did ask the farmers to indicate their memberships in organizations, the extent of their contacts outside the community, the number of neighbors they visited, and the average number of trips they made in a year to the nearest big city.

THE RESEARCH FINDINGS

The Rate of Diffusion

If the annual number of farmers trying hybrid corn for the first time is plotted over a ten-year period, the graph is roughly S-shaped (Figure 1). This indicates that there was an early period when a few pioneering farmers tried out the innovation. Then followed a rapid middle period when many other farmers adopted the seed, and finally a late period when even die-hard traditionalists accepted the new idea. The shape of the curve implies that most farmers accepted the new seed only after hearing about its results from their friends and neighbors.

By contrast, the curve showing the acceptance of gammanym among doctors shows a very rapid state of adoption right after the drug was introduced. This is followed by a very steep, almost straight, line to a peak eight months later (Figure 2). Almost two-thirds of the doctors wrote their first prescription for the new medicine in the first eight months.

FIGURE 1

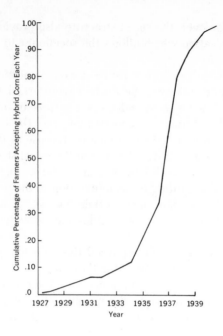

FIGURE 2

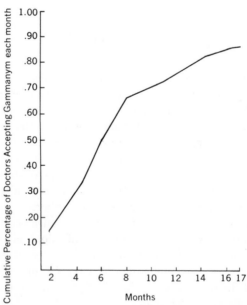

The most striking difference between the two curves is the lack of any early, slow, testing period among the doctors such as the farmers showed. Perhaps this only reflects the greater conservatism and cautiousness of farmers. Or, perhaps, it is simply because corn planting takes at least a year to prove itself.

Yet, despite the apparent difference, the acceptance rate of the drug still provides some strong support for the finding first revealed in the research on the new type of corn—that personal relationships and personal recommendations are the most important part of the process of diffusion.

This can be seen in Figure 3, where the curve of adoption of the drug has been shown for the integrated (or most popular) doctors, those of average popularity, and the isolated (or least popular) doctors. (This classification provided a rigorous test which was not used on the farmers.) The curve of the most popular doctors shoots almost straight up before leveling off. By contrast, the curve of the least popular doctors climbs slowly and steadily at an almost constant rate. And the curve of those of average popularity falls between the other two.

FIGURE 3

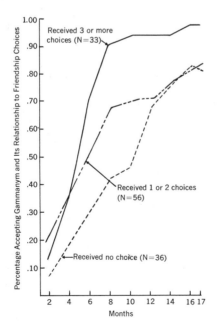

The curve of the integrated doctors shows a chain reaction pattern. In other words, one popular doctor tried the drug and told several friends about its results. Each of these friends tried it and told several of *their* friends, who then did the same. The curve probably reached its peak when all the popular doctors had told all their friends. In short, integrated doctors with many friends and close colleagues were most influenced by personal contacts—just as were the farmers.

On the other hand, the curve of the isolated doctors shows that an almost equal proportion adopted gammanym each month. This means that some constant influence, such as an advertising campaign, reached a roughly equal number of doctors each month and influenced their decision to try the drug.

Innovation on the Installment Plan

The first doctors and farmers to try out the new product were very conservative; they usually tested small amounts in the first years. Thus the farmers' acreage in hybrid corn averaged 20 percent in the first year. It reached 25 percent in the fifth year and 69 percent in the seventh year.

In the same way the doctors wrote an average of 1.5 prescriptions in a three-day period in the first two months when gammanym was used and 2.7 prescriptions in a three-day period four months later.

The first users served as testers for the entire community. However, as more and more of the doctors and farmers began to use the new products, the later adopters among them became bolder and bolder.

Information Is Not Enough

Could it be that the late adopters did not use the new products earlier because they lacked adequate information? That is not a true explanation.

Ryan and Gross found that while it took 13 years before every single farmer had heard about the new kind of corn, almost 60 percent had heard about it within three years. More important, while over 90 percent of the farmers had heard about the new corn within seven years, only 20 percent had tried it by that time.

The time gap between hearing and using was much shorter

among the doctors; yet a similar lag occurred. Although two-thirds of the doctors had read or heard about the wonder drug within four months of its introduction, only about one-third of the doctors had actually used it by then.

WHICH COMMUNICATIONS CHANNELS ARE MOST INFLUENTIAL?

If simply getting the word is not enough, what, then, convinces an individual to accept a new idea?

About half the farmers reported that a salesman brought them the first word about the new seed (Table 1). The drug

TABLE 1
Sources of Knowledge of Hybrid Seed Corn

	PERCENT OF FARM OPERATORS CREDITING SOURCE WITH	
	ORIGINAL KNOWLEDGE	MOST INFLUENCE
Salesmen	49%	32%
Neighbors and Relatives	18	50
Farm Journals	11	2
Radio Advertising	10	—
Extension Service	3	2
All Other Media	9	14
Total	100	100
Total Number of Farmers	(257)	(257)

company's salesman and the drug company's mailed advertisements in the same way played a part in informing doctors about the new drug (Table 2). Yet while salesmen may have brought the first word, farmers, and particularly doctors, heard from a

TABLE 2

Sources of Knowledge of Gammanym

	PERCENT OF PHYSICIANS CREDITING SOURCE WITH	
	ORIGINAL KNOWLEDGE	MOST INFLUENCE
Salesmen	57%	38%
Colleagues	7	20
Direct Mail	18	8
Drug House Periodicals	4	5
Journal Articles	7	23
Meetings	3	—
All Other Media	4	6
Total	100	100
Total Number of Physicians	(141)	(141)

variety of sources including official and expert opinion before they finally took action (Table 3).

Thus the diffusion of innovation apparently depends on two different channels of communication: the introductory channels and the activating channels. Salesmen (introducers) were credited with informing doctors and farmers, but neighbors and colleagues (activators) were credited with actually convincing them. The introducers help the spread of information, but the activators help the spread of conviction.

WHO ARE THE EARLY ADOPTERS?

But who, or what, first influences the friends who do the convincing?

Apparently, in every society there are natural pioneers, men who are willing to try new ideas and who are capable of convincing the others, the majority, by their example. They are the

TABLE 3

Sequence of Sources of Information about Gammanym

	PERCENT OF PHYSICIANS CREDITING SOURCE WITH	
	ORIGINAL KNOWLEDGE	LAST ADDITIONAL INFORMATION PRIOR TO ADOPTION
Salesmen	52%	5%
Colleagues and Meetings	13	36
Direct Mail	22	14
Journal Articles	6	21
Drug House Periodicals	3	21
All Other Media	4	3
Total	100	100
Total Mentions *	(87)	(87)

* The modal physician named three or more sources of information. This table includes only the 87 who mentioned three or more sources.

"opinion leaders." And the diffusion of innovation depends on the "two-step flow" of information through them to the general public. In short, a message is received by the opinion leader, who tries it, and then convinces other members of the community by argument or by example.

The opinion leaders are a special breed. The research team found that the doctors who first accepted gammanym were, for example, those who subscribed to more medical journals, went to more out-of-town medical conventions, visited other medical institutions, and consulted with more out-of-town experts on special cases.

The sociologists studying farmers found similar patterns. The pioneering users of hybrid corn usually were younger, better educated, and less bound to traditions of old-time farming. The early adopters among the farmers visited Des Moines, the nearest big city, 4.5 times a year, while the average late adopters usually visited the big town only 1.5 times a year. Contact with the outside world is an important characteristic of the innovator.

In conclusion, when farmers and seeds are compared with doctors and drugs, personal recommendation is found to be by far the most influential factor in the spread of a new idea.

Moreover, both studies found that information is not enough. The majority of doctors and farmers would not accept an innovation merely because of hearing about it. Conversations with friends and colleagues were what finally convinced them.

Both studies also found that the early adopter—the man most likely to accept new ideas—usually had many contacts within his own field as well as many interests in the world outside.

These findings have provided basic guidelines for the public relations and advertising professions. Almost every professional organizer of a campaign or drive uses the "two-step flow" concept: he seeks to reach opinion leaders who then will set the trend for the rest of the community. However, in one particular the doctors were not like the farmers. Although both were active in their professional organizations, the early adopting doctor was usually well integrated in the community of doctors. But the early adopting farmer was not as likely to be a man who played an active role in an informal circle of friends.

Of course, this difference may be explained by the fact that innovating in medicine is risky. A doctor may be unwilling to try out a new drug without being sure he knows all its effects. As a result, in talking and consulting other doctors and in trying out the new medicine together with them and comparing results, he grows less uneasy. If the report of the new product is good, he grows confident and will begin to prescribe it. On the other hand, the farmer, independent in opinion, can try out a new seed or new technique without risk to anyone but himself.

Katz points out that, on the whole, the doctors in the study seemed all more favorably disposed to try out new things than the farmers, who shared no such norm. He therefore reasons that the sociable, popular doctor, being the one to follow his group's values, would thus be an innovator. But the popular farmer might not become an innovator if his group did not particularly value experimentation.

Fashion: The Rhythm of Change*

Does the study of fashion show that culture must be studied in its own right in place of studying the actions of the individual members of society?

Does culture operate in an orderly fashion in accordance with laws of its own?

Is fashion the result of (a) efforts of an elite group to set itself apart from groups which it considers socially inferior, or (b) efforts of commercial groups, seeking to set and control the direction of fashion, or (c) a process of selecting from competing models those which best reflect the emerging tastes of the mass?

Does fashion function to bring order amid many divergent choices in a rapidly changing area of social life?

Year after year, especially each spring when the bills from the dress shop reached their annual high-water mark, Dorothy Jarvis would hear her husband groan: "Why must women be such slaves to fashion?" And year after year, she would parry his accusation by asking: "Do you or don't you want me to be in style?" Dorothy realized, of course, that her husband, Jim, would be the first to complain if she appeared in public looking like last year's leftover. So, in a sense, they were both slaves to fashion.

Dorothy seldom read the glossy fashion magazines and took little interest in the latest whims in feminine wearing apparel. Yet because she did not want to be called dowdy or old-fashioned, she forced herself to notice the major fashion trends and kept a particularly sharp eye out for rising or falling hemlines. In this manner, for over 40 years, she had found herself caught up in the

---

* Adapted from "On the Principle of Order in Civilization as Exemplified by Changes in Fashion" by A. L. Kroeber, *American Anthropologist,* Vol. 21, No. 3 (1919), pp. 239–260; also adapted from "Fashion: From Class Differentiation to Collective Selection" by Herbert Blumer, *Sociological Quarterly,* Vol. 10, No. 3 (Summer 1969), pp. 277–290. Reprinted by permission.

"revolutions" of fashion of each decade and, to a lesser extent, in the minor "revolts" of every two or three years.

In the late 1920s, for instance, she had gone in for the "flapper" look, with its daringly high skirts, low waists, and hats that fitted low around the face. In the thirties, she had loyally changed to the long skirts and severely tailored suits of the Depression era. In the wartime forties, skirts had crept back up, and, like all the other women, Dorothy had worn peasant dirndls, padded shoulders, snoods, and wedgies. She had followed the "New Look" of the late forties, when skirts returned to nearly ankle length. In the conservative fifties, she had raised her hemlines again and clothed herself in "basic black." Finally, in the swinging sixties, she had switched still another time when the mini-skirt burst upon the scene together with wild prints and "costumes" inspired by Bonnie and Clyde, revolutionary Russia, turn-of-the-century art, the cowboy-and-Indian era, and the Edwardian dandies. Hemlines were right back where they had been in the twenties.

Dorothy could only conclude that women were indeed slaves of fashion. But who were the masters? She thought that it must be the dress designers and clothing manufacturers. Their livelihoods depended on creating a demand for new things, and they personally benefited from every radical turnover in style.

A. L. Kroeber, an anthropologist who began scientifically investigating the meaning of fashion over 50 years ago, would not have agreed with Dorothy. He considered fashion seriously, as a force that made people act alike, that is, that led to uniformities in behavior.

The most obvious forces causing people to act alike are law and custom. Laws are made deliberately and then changed deliberately by lawmakers, acting for society as a whole. Custom is not set up or changed in so formal a manner, and in this respect fashion is like custom. People act as "fashion dictates," but they do it as individuals, one by one of their own free will. They do not call together a congress or a public meeting to decide what fashions to take up. When beards became stylish among American youths, they did not convene to agree to grow beards; yet great numbers of youths did grow them.

Voluntary uniformities of this sort are what fascinated Kroeber. Some of his fellow social scientists in 1919 thought the subject was foolish. Yet Kroeber's report not only made fashion the theme of serious study; it still stands as a respected and valid work on a fascinating aspect of human behavior. He would answer Dorothy's question by pointing out that, far from determining the larger revolutions in fashion, the dress designers themselves follow long-term trends over which they have very little control.

KROEBER'S DATA

The changes in fashion may appear on the surface to be sudden, fanciful, and meaningless. However, Kroeber observed that over long periods of time certain orderly principles were at work. In other words, it was possible to trace the origin, growth, climax, decline, and death of a fashion just as it was possible to trace the life cycle of an organism. To prove this theory and to discover just what these orderly principles were, Kroeber undertook to study the changing styles in women's dresses over a period of 75 years. We may suppose he picked female dress because it changes more than does male attire.

This is how he went about his unorthodox research project: For his source materials Kroeber turned to the illustrations of models in the fashion magazines. He began with 1844 because that was the date of the oldest fashion monthly he could find: the French *Petit Courier des Dames*. He studied the pictures in it and in *Harper's Bazaar* and *Vogue*, two American magazines for women, until 1919.

He confined his comparisons to clothing of a single type—women's full evening dress. This type of dress had served the same purpose for over a century and had not been affected by any fundamentally new concepts. Therefore, the variations would be purely matters of style. Thus, if any principle could be determined, it would apply even more forcefully to more changeable kinds of clothing such as street and office wear.

Kroeber tabulated and compared eight basic measurements of the magazine models. They included a figure which he used as a base line, namely:

the total length of the model's figure from the center of the mouth to the tip of the toe, or, if the shoes were covered, to the lowest point of the skirt edge;

the distance from the mouth to the bottom of the skirt;

the diameter of the skirt at its hem or base;

the diameter of the skirt at the point where it was greatest, in cases where skirts swelled, narrowed, then flared again.

Four other measurements included the length and diameter of the waist and the depth and breadth of the decolletage (the opening at the neck). He measured ten magazine figures in these eight ways in each calendar year from 1844 to 1919. Then he converted the measurements into percentages of his base measurement—the length of the entire figure. The percentages for each measure were then averaged for each year. It is these averages of the percentages for each year that appear in the graphs that follow.

WIDTH OF SKIRT

Did Kroeber detect any underlying principles amidst the mountains of measurements he took? One immediately struck him as he plotted the course of skirt diameters from 1844 to 1919 (Figure 1). The graph plainly shows that despite minor fluctuations, the dominating trend during 60 of the 75 years studied was toward ever narrower skirts. The dotted line across the middle of the graph marks 65.3, the figure which stood for the average of skirt widths throughout the 75 years. The line helps to show the crests and troughs of the "waves." Roughly speaking, in the first half of this period skirts grew wider, and in the second half they grew slimmer, but always with small temporary setbacks.

The first few years shown in Figure 1 can be considered merely a prelude to the unfolding of the great skirt-width drama. When the story began in 1844, for instance, the diameters of evening dresses stood at a moderate 57 percent of body length. The percentage rose gradually at first. Then, after 1851, it began to mount rapidly and continuously until it reached the maximum of 116 in 1859. This was the apex of the crinoline hoop skirt

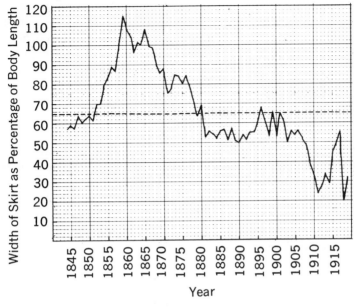

FIGURE 1

fashion, when the flare of the skirt exceeded the height of the woman wearing it. But from 1859 on, for 50 years, skirt diameters became progressively narrower.

Smaller reactions culminated in 1865 and 1872 and violent fluctuations occurred in the years from 1896 to 1903. As can be seen in Figure 1, the upward climb from 1851 to 1859 is matched by the downward trend between 1865 and 1871. From 1880 to 1905, skirt widths normally hovered between 50 and 70 percent of the total length of the figure.

After 1908, however, the character of the long-term trend became unmistakable. Women began squeezing themselves into the very tight hobble and tube skirts toward which fashion had evidently been heading for a full half century. By 1911 the extreme of slimness was reached: Skirt widths totaled only 23 percent of the whole figure—less than half the narrowest dimension attained in the 60 preceding years and but a fifth of the greatest width.

But in the years 1912–1917, skirts began widening again. The trend was not altered by the fashions of 1918 and 1919 which should be interpreted as nothing more than temporary reactions. Thus, on the basis of the 75-year period he studied and of his general knowledge of earlier historical eras, Kroeber concluded that from 50 to 60 years was the average duration of trends in skirt widths—a rhythm that would probably not be broken unless there was some radical change in fashion such as the present-day substitution of formal pants for skirts.

LENGTH OF SKIRT

Each measurement has its own principle of order. The rhythms of skirt length are only about a third of the rhythms of skirt width: 35 years as against 100 years (Figure 2). Thus, evening gowns were worn at full length between 1860 and 1875 and again between 1900 and 1910. Likewise, formal dresses entered a shortening phase in the period 1876–1887 and again in 1911–1919.

There is another difference between widths and lengths: The width of a skirt can become infinitely voluminous because it has

(1) Length of Skirt;   (2) Length of Waist;   (3) Decolletage

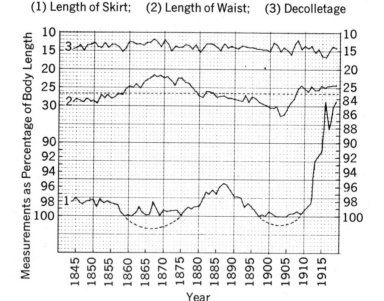

FIGURE 2

no natural boundaries—except, possibly, the wearer's convenience and the size of the ballroom. But skirt lengths are of necessity fixed. A skirt can only drop to the floor and no farther. Similarly, if skirt lengths reach too far above the knee, the skirt of a dress will cease to be a skirt and become instead a blouse—the shirt dress and the "mini," which actually set in, in 1969. For this reason, when skirt lengths are longest, they remain *apparently* stationary for a time. But when skirt lengths attain a minimum, they reach a climax and quickly descend again.

Still another principle is at work in skirt lengths. In Kroeber's 75-year period, each fashion trend, in general, lasted a shorter time than the trend before it. Styles in length altered more rapidly and unrestrainedly as time went on. Thus, the plotted curves are like swinging seesaws in the twentieth century and like moderate slopes in the nineteenth century (Figure 2).

In the same way, Kroeber followed the movements of fashion in depth of neckline (Figure 2). Here the trends resembled the trends in the widths of skirts. And when he measured the expanse of exposed shoulder (that is, width of neckline), he discovered that the greater the area of bare shoulder, the higher the neck of the dress. There was clear evidence of a 70-year trend toward boldness in depth of necklines but modesty in breadth.

ORDER OR ANARCHY?

What is most captivating in fashion is the endless procession of novelties, innovations, and alterations. The details—the trimmings, pleats and ruffles, buttons and bows, colors and materials, all the eye-catching characteristics of dress—do, in fact, change very rapidly. And it is the essence of fashion to play these up. Consequently, one is likely to believe that the only principle at work in fashion is chaos and that there are no regularities.

However, underneath the bewildering maze of detail, the major proportions in dress styles change slowly and solemnly. To Kroeber, this suggested that here there was, after all, something resembling law at work. In other words, certain features in fashion change according to a scheme, and the underlying pattern, or order of things, can be discovered.

This does not mean that Kroeber was confident that he could forecast the fashions of the future on the basis of his investigations of one 75-year period. On the contrary: A research worker might have to familiarize himself with the fashions of 250 years, 500 years, or even 1000 or more years before all the patterns or rhythms became clear. But Kroeber concluded that some forecast could be made of the future course of any one basic element in style whose history had been sufficiently investigated.

How much study is sufficient is really the question. For styles and their cycles cannot be understood except in relation to civilization as a whole. Likewise, the rate of cultural change in the society as a whole must be understood. How does this rate affect the *rate* of change in the world of fashion? For example, if fashions were examined over a 2000-year span, it might be discovered that styles remained relatively stable during those centuries when basic change was slow and when trade, commerce, and the exchange of ideas were limited. However, as the rate of change accelerated in Western Europe beginning in the sixteenth century, the duration of each successive style—at least in the long run—could be expected to become shorter and shorter. Indeed,

(1865)

CROWD AND MASS BEHAVIOR

(1897) (1910) (1920)

(1950's) (1969) (1970)

Kroeber attached great importance to his discovery that his measurements showed more rapid and more extreme variations in the last 25 years of his survey than they did in the preceding half-century. This movement, as he suggested, matched the general quickening pace of social change in the western world.

Kroeber pointed to a connection between the laws at work in fashion and the more general forces in society, but he did not actually explain how fashion responds to these social forces. The nature of these social forces has been studied by Herbert Blumer, a sociologist at the University of California at Berkeley. His theory is presented in the pages which follow.

Blumer interprets fashion as representing, for one thing, a deliberate and rational choice on the part of those adopting it, not as a collective craze. For another, he sees it as an important form of social control, not as an inconsequential social happening. And, finally, he identifies the operation of fashion in many fields, not just in clothing and adornment.

How does fashion move through society? In certain primitive societies, fashion changes so slowly that one might think people simply wear the same costume for generations without end. But their dress and decoration do change, as do their other art styles. In more complex societies, however, fashion often serves to differentiate the upper classes from the lower classes. If it is an open society, those below will strive to imitate those above by adopting their mode of dress. This, in turn, spurs the elite into devising new styles that will proclaim their superior status and keep up their prestige. Thus a cycle of shifting fashions begins, with the change to new styles coming from above and filtering downward. This is probably the way fashion operated throughout much of European history. Class-structured society, which allowed for some upward mobility, together with a relatively slow place of social change, determined fashion's relatively slow movement.

In more democratic and rapidly changing societies, however, an emphasis on modernity, or up-to-dateness, takes the place of prestige in determining the direction that fashion will take. It moves today through the medium of the fashion industry. The dress designers create the new styles. But they cannot control how they will be received. Their ideas are derived principally from three sources: from models culled from the past and the exotic; from current and recent styles; and, in particular, from the most recent expressions of modernity in the fine arts, literature, films, music, politics, and the world of the sophisticated—the "Beautiful People" as they were called in the late 1960s.

From the hundreds of creations produced annually by any one fashion house, the department store buyers select only a few models. These will be the ones that ultimately appear for sale in the mass market. But to survive in their jobs, the buyers themselves must guess well, for they must be able to sense the direction of the public's taste. Thus both designers and buyers are dependent on the tastes taking shape in the mind of the fashion-consuming public.

New styles do not emerge because the elite embraces them. Rather, it is the suitability or potential fashionableness of the design which encourages the elite to lend its prestige to it. Actually, it is the innovator who is responsible for bringing new styles to the fore—and innovators are not always the people with the most prestige. In fact, in recent years, some of the most important fashion innovations in America have come from the ranks of the least privileged—the young, the black, and the outcast.

Proof of the fact that prestige or power alone cannot control the direction of fashion is seen in the unsuccessful attempt of the clothing manufacturers, designers, fashion magazines, and acknowledged fashion leaders to reverse the trend toward shorter skirts which started in 1919 and went on until 1929. A similar campaign late in 1968 and in 1969 and 1970 to dampen the mass enthusiasm for miniskirts also was a partial failure.

What is involved here is a sort of collective groping for what is "in," or will soon be "in," among certain groups or individuals who express the emerging tastes or interests of an era. Thus, in women's dress, taste will respond not only to whatever trends are already established but also to the latest developments in fabrics and ornamentation, to new experiments in the arts, to exciting public events, and to political happenings. Taste responds, too, to major social shifts such as the emancipation of women, the growing consciousness of black people, and the emergence of the youth culture.* This responsiveness brings fashion into line with the overall direction of modernity itself, in short, with the "spirit of the times."

Personal appearance became a matter of overriding importance in the youth culture in the late 1960s in the United States. The youth culture's elites—the student leaders, the black leaders and the hippie cultists—launched the fashions of long hair, "Afros," beards, beads, sandals, dashikis, ponchos, fringed jackets, and of flower decals in psychedelic colors plastered all over their cars and motorcycles. By following the elites' styles, their followers show they are "with it." Just as in "high fashion," each item is in some way inspired by events and personalities which attract the attention of the mass. The Afros and dashikis originate in Third World enthusiasms; sandals go with the popularity of Zen Buddhism and other Oriental systems of thought; flower decals probably come from drug-induced experience; ponchos identify the wearers with Che Guevera.

Often, once a new fashion has been adopted, it seems to compel adherence, at least for a period of time. Thus the role of fashion may be to aid the collective adjustment of society to a changing world. First, fashion introduces a measure of uniformity where there would otherwise be chaos. By fostering unanimity and order, fashion thus performs in a rapidly changing society a function which custom performs in a settled society.

Second, fashion serves to detach the grip of the past. By placing value on being "up to date" and scorning older forms, it frees the way for movement in new directions. Finally, it helps prepare people for the immediate future.

Thus, Dorothy Jarvis grumbles, but she follows the fashions just the same. Her independent choice, however, has the effect of helping to unify society, at least in appearances. Dressed in the latest style, Dorothy feels "with it." In a society in which unity is threatened by change and authority is constantly challenged, fashion gives the individual a sense of belonging. But if Dorothy is a slave to fashion, her real master is society itself.

---

* See "Middle-Class Delinquency" in *Delinquents and Criminals: Their Social World* in this *Readings in Sociology* Series.

The Spread of a Social Contagion*

What is meant by social contagion?

How may it show itself?

What was the state of mind of a group of workers in a plant who were affected by an hysterical rash?

Did the rash affect all the individuals?

What is the role of the group's leaders in the contagious outbreak?

How do the social networks between workers who are friends affect the spread of the contagion?

How are the social isolates affected?

What put an end to the hysterical behavior?

McKinnon's is a medium-sized clothing manufacturing plant in the South where raw fibers are spun, dyed, and woven and the finished cloth then cut, sewn, boxed, and shipped to wholesale and retail outlets. It employs a few hundred people, mostly women, and operates on two shifts.

In the summer of 1962 McKinnon's ran into trouble. Even before the trouble began there was an air of tension about the place. The women had worked overtime day after day. The plant was not well organized, and the women felt unsure of their jobs. They feared they would be laid off when the peak season was over. Then, in one week, the entire company was thrown into an uproar by an epidemic of insect bites which, before running its course, incapacitated 62 people.

The first person to complain of symptoms was a young girl from a distant rural area who had worked at McKinnon's only a short time and was virtually unknown to any of the other em-

* Adapted from "Sociometric Patterns in Hysterical Contagion" by Alan C. Kerckhoff, Kurt W. Back, and Norman Miller, *Sociometry*, Vol. 28, No. 1 (March 1965), pp. 2–15. Reprinted by permission.

ployees. For this reason, nobody paid much attention to what she said. The second person to complain was a much older woman who had worked in the plant many years, but she had few acquaintances' among the predominantly younger girls who made up the bulk of the work force. She, too, was largely ignored.

But the third person bitten was a very popular young woman. Her case aroused the sympathy and fears of everyone who worked near her. After that, people began to talk openly of the insects and of the unclean conditions in the plant which, they complained, threatened their health. And as several more women reported alarming symptoms, the talk grew louder and longer.

Within four days, ten persons were struck, their symptoms ranging from minor irritations of the skin to fainting spells, severe pain, nausea, or feelings of disorientation. The contagion spread so fast, in fact, that on the two worst days, 24 and 20 persons, respectively, came down with the symptoms. Then just as suddenly, the complaints began to diminish—only four people reported insect bites after that.

With the visit of the exterminator, who sprayed the premises for bugs, the epidemic was considered halted. But while the epidemic had lasted, it had seriously disrupted operations in the plant, and had caused financial losses to both management and workers.

What is strange is that although the 62 persons affected had received medical treatment, their condition could not be attributed to physical causes. Both a physician and an entomologist (insect specialist) from the Communicable Disease Center in Atlanta, Georgia, had visited the plant during the crisis. However, they were unable to find any poisonous element capable of causing the reported symptoms, even though they had searched for insects and other possible causes, such as chemical irritants in the dyes or in the air conditioning system.

All they knew was that almost all the victims were women; almost all were white; almost all worked on the first shift; and almost all worked within one specific area of the plant. From this, they could only conclude that the "epidemic" of bites and pains had originated entirely in the minds of the victims, not in the physical conditions of the plant itself. Those who were bitten, in short, were victims of an hysterical delusion. The anxieties caused by overwork, pressure, fatigue, and the prospect of losing their jobs in the near future had made them easy prey to this condition.

Hysterical contagion is a subject of scientific interest to Alan C. Kerckhoff and Kurt W. Back of Duke University and to Norman Miller of the University of Chicago. It is an important form of collective behavior whch has left its mark on many periods of history.* But the question of greatest concern to these three sociologists is whether social relations established by hysterical people have any bearing on the spread of contagion. In other words, do an individual's friendships (or lack of friendships) or an individual's place in a group have any effect on whether he or she will exhibit hysterical symptoms or not? And does the individual's place in a group tend to speed up or slow down the spread of hysteria in that group? To find out, they turned to the case of hysteria that had taken place in the southern factory and there measured the interpersonal relations of all those who were involved.

THE SAMPLE

This is how they went about their study: They first drew a 25 percent sample of all the women in the plant who worked on the first shift. They then added to this list all those women who had been affected by "the bug" but who had not been drawn in the sample. This gave them a total of 185 subjects, of whom 58 were affected cases and 127 were "controls." Each of these women was then asked by an interviewer to name her three best friends in the plant. The picture of friendships revealed by the women's answers showed where the most used lines of communication among them probably lay.

These methods gave the sociologists three vital bits of information: (1) the pattern of relationships enjoyed by each woman; (2) exactly which subjects had been affected and which had not; and (3) the date on which each affected case had been "bitten." To simplify their analysis, they distributed the 58 af-

* See "Forms of Crowd and Mass Behavior" in this book.

fected cases in four categories: (1) those "bitten" before the two biggest days of the "epidemic" (ten women); (2) those affected on Day One, or the first big day of the crisis (24 women); (3) those affected on Day Two (20 women); and (4) those affected after these two days (four women).

The investigators wanted to know specifically whether the friendships the women had developed in the plant had influenced the spread of the hysterical symptoms within the population. They wished to test three possible theories: (1) that those who were linked together by friendship would be more likely to be affected; (2) that those who were outside a network of friendly relations would be more likely to be affected; and (3) that the pattern of social relations, whatever it was, would not be connected in any way with the spread of the symptoms.

The first theory, which can be dubbed the "group influence theory," assumes that individuals will behave like other members of their group when the group is consistent in how it defines, or interprets, a situation. That is, people will "see" or "feel" what their neighbors believe they are seeing or feeling and then respond accordingly. However, with respect to this theory, it must be remembered that in the southern plant the majority of workers never exhibited any hysterical symptoms. Thus, those who wanted to resist the contagion could always have found other workers whose more sensible behavior could have served as a model for them.

The second, or "social isolation," theory assumes that social isolates, or friendless people, are more likely to "catch" the hysterical contagion than are people who are better adjusted socially. For instance, the average worker in the factory would have had at least some social contacts with persons who did not exhibit any hysterical symptoms, since they were in the majority. Therefore the average worker would have known that some people denied the seriousness of the insect threat. But the social isolate, in contrast, would not have been in a position to know that anyone thought his notions and conduct strange or undesirable. Furthermore, if hysterical behavior is looked upon as an attention-getting device, then social isolates can be expected to indulge in it, for they need attention more than those who have social ties. Finally, the outcast, the person with few ties to the social system,

CROWD AND MASS BEHAVIOR

is a more likely candidate than others to take part in all forms of collective behavior.

The third, or "crowd response," theory assumes that the social relationships (or lack of social relationships) among the people in question have no bearing on the spread of hysteria. In other words, the contagion spreads by a sort of "magic," a magic that appeals to various individuals for their own private reasons but that does not depend on their knowing each other beforehand. After yielding to the "magic," those exhibiting the hysteric behavior may identify themselves with each other for they feel that they have something in common. But this happens purely as a result of their shared experience in the crowd. In the factory situation, the fact that all those affected by hysteria were fellow-workers (and the great majority of them women) would have been ground enough for this sense of identification.

Each one of these theoretical positions, the sociologists point out, is plausible; but since they appear to be mutually contradictory, they could not all be correct—in fact, no two of them could be correct. And yet, impossible as it may seem, Kerckhoff, Back, and Miller maintain that all three of them are correct. Here is their evidence:

THE TEST OF THE HYPOTHESES

When they looked at the overall differences between affected cases and controls (without considering the date on which a woman was affected), the group influence theory seemed to be borne out (Table 1). First, there were fewer social isolates or friendless women among the affected workers than there were among the controls: 28 percent as against 33 percent. The affected women were chosen as friends somewhat more often than were the unaffected women (averaging 1.4 times as against 1.2). At any rate, there was certainly no general tendency for the hysterical women to be socially excluded.

Furthermore,.affected women were more than twice as likely to name other affected women as their friends than they were to name controls as their friends (57 percent as against 26 percent). That ties of friendship bound the bitten women to each other is shown by the percentages of mutual choices. The hysterical

TABLE 1
Choices Among Affected Cases and Controls

CHARACTERISTIC	TOTAL SAMPLE	
	AFFECTED	CONTROL
Total Number	58	127
Average number of times a woman was chosen as friend	1.4	1.2
Percent of cases who are isolates	28%	33%
Percent of choices naming affected women	⎡27%⎤*	⎡9%⎤*
Percent of choices naming controls	⎣25 ⎦	⎣28 ⎦
Percent chosen by affected women only	⎡31⎤*	⎡13⎤*
Percent chosen by controls only	⎣21⎦	⎣43⎦
Percent of choices named by affected women	57%	26%
Percent of choices named by controls	43	74
Total	100	100
Percent of mutual choices with affected women	59	30
Percent of mutual choices with controls	41	30
Total	100	100

* Percentages do not total 100 because choices could be made of unaffected persons in other parts of the plant but not in the sample.

women were twice as likely, in fact, to be chosen as friends solely by other "bitten" women (59 percent, contrasted with 30 percent). And the controls were twice as likely to be chosen exclusively by women who had not been "bitten" (70 percent, contrasted with 41 percent).

Thus, the sociologists concluded that the hysterical women were not only part of a social network but that they were linked together much more closely than they were to women who did not become affected. This seemed to be evidence that the contagion followed social channels, in other words, that it was influenced by the group.

However, when they started analyzing the affected category only, according to the period in which the women became affected, some new facts shed light on the spread of the affliction (Table 2). When they looked at the first cases to exhibit the hysterical symptoms (the "before" category), they found that 50 percent of them were social isolates. By contrast no more than 25 percent of the cases occurring in any of the later periods were isolates. This was also reflected in the fact that on the average, affected women were chosen as friends by others oftener in the two big periods, "Day One" and "Day Two," than they had been at the outset, "Before."

They also found that the later a woman was affected, the more likely she was to be chosen by other affected women (40 percent "Before"; 58 percent on "Day One"; and 63 percent on "Day Two"). Correspondingly, the later they were "bitten," the less likely were affected women to be chosen only by controls (60, 43, and 37 percent). In other words, as time went on, there appeared to be an increasing tendency for the hysterical contagion to settle within one social network, to the exclusion of other networks. Thus, the pattern in the early phase is in keeping with the theory of social isolation. But the pattern during the major portion of the epidemic is in keeping with the theory of group influence.

Does this mean that the sociologists had to reject the theory of crowd response? Not at all. When they examined the four cases in the "after" phase, they found still another picture of how the contagion had operated. The women in this small group were chosen as a best friend on an average of 1.5 times, a record comparable to the "Day One" (1.7) and "Day Two" (1.3) women. However, in contrast to the clannishness of the women who were affected at the height of the epidemic, only 18 percent of the friends chosen by these late joiners came from among the ranks of the affected and only half of the women who chose them in turn came from the affected category. Furthermore, when it was a matter of mutual choices, two out of three of the "after" choices were among controls. This was evidence of the spread of the epi-

TABLE 2

Choices Among Affected Cases

CHARACTERISTIC	"BEFORE"	"DAY ONE"	"DAY TWO"
Total Number	10	24	20
Average number of times a woman chosen as friend	1.0	1.7	1.3
Percent of cases who are isolates	50%	21%	25%
Percent of choices naming affected women	27% *	31% *	25% *
Percent of choices naming controls	23	29	21
Percent chosen by affected women only	10 *	29 *	45 *
Percent chosen by controls only	20	21	15
Percent of choices named by affected women	40%	58%	63%
Percent of choices named by controls	60	43	37
Total	100	101†	100
Percent of mutual choices among affected women	50	61	63
Percent of mutual choices among controls	50	39	38
Total	100	100	101†

* Percentages do not total 100 because choices may be made of unaffected persons in other parts of the plant but not in the sample.
† Total exceeds 100 percent because of rounding of figures to nearest decimal.

demic to persons who had more social ties outside the affected category than inside it.

The fact that these last few cases were distributed in a more haphazard way could be interpreted simply as the spread of the contagion to a new social group that had not previously been involved. But it could also be argued that at this point the epidemic was no longer being carried through regular social channels at all, that it was in fact becoming a general reaction. In other words, a "crowd response" was setting in—just at the moment when the entire epidemic was brought to a halt by the arrival of the exterminator and the insistence of the experts that the hysteria was unwarranted.

CONCLUSIONS

From their data, the sociologists came to the following conclusions about the nature of contagion. Their explanation of it requires drawing upon all three of the theories which they tested. An epidemic, such as the one which took place in the southern plant, begins when one or more persons, because of certain peculiarities of temperament or character, exhibit symptoms which then become the model for at least a limited number of others in the same situation. At first, those most likely to follow this lead are isolates, who are not very well adjusted socially. Thus, the social groups that do exist may view the new form of behavior as objectionable or unworthy of attention.

However, as a number of other persons follow the lead, it is increasingly likely that some who are part of a group will also be affected. These people, who are pivotal in the spread of the contagion, may well be somewhat unusual emotionally, or perhaps particularly anxious about something. Yet it is through just such channels that the contagion enters regular social networks and then starts spreading with greater and greater rapidity in a sort of chain reaction. In short, the influence of insiders puts the stamp of approval on behavior which otherwise would probably not be taken up. With numbers to bolster it, the abnormal behavior begins to seem normal. Members of the group have reached the point where they really believe that there is something, like a bug, which threatens them.

Once the abnormal behavior has been accepted as normal, it is adopted at a much faster rate within the social groups where it has caught on than outside them. Compared to "in" group members, outsiders are thereafter slower to respond. However, as more and more people start behaving in the new way, the sheer size of the affected group makes the hysterical behavior and the explanation given for it seem fairly convincing. In time, "just about everyone" comes to believe in the bug. After that, cases begin to occur in scattered, unrelated segments of the population and eventually throughout the entire plant. It thus becomes a crowd response.

Through this explanation, the sociologists bring about a meeting of the three different theories they started out with. They show how each theory is true up to a point and how each contributes to a fuller understanding of the total pattern of hysterical contagion.

The Making of the President: 1940 and 1960*

How do people decide to vote in an election?

When a voter is making up his mind between one candidate and another, how may other people's opinions affect his choice?

What was the impact of the televised debates between Kennedy and Nixon on (a) the viewers' images of the candidates and on (b) the viewers' voting intentions?

How much influence do the candidates' images have on the voter?

Or, how much does the voter's intention influence his image of the candidates?

How do persons resolve contradictions between their voting intention and their image of the candidates?

The reporting of research on the election of 1940 was the first study of its kind. It came at a time of vigorous political activity. The New Deal, already introduced by President Franklin Roosevelt, was arousing violent feeling on the home front. In addition, with Europe already at war, the issue of involvement in a foreign war became a dominating question in the minds of voters. Thus, public interest in the election of 1940 was intense. Nearly 50 million votes were cast. (Four years later, when Franklin Roosevelt ran against Thomas Dewey, fewer than 48 million voted.)

The following reading first presents the findings concerning the election of 1940 and then compares such findings with studies made of the election of 1960. By then, television had brought a new factor into the political process.

* Adapted from *The People's Choice* by Paul F. Lazarsfeld, Bernard Berelson, and Hazel Gaudet (New York: Columbia University Press, 1944 and 1968), pp. 52–53, 55–57, 59–66, 69; also from "Ordeal by Debate: Viewer Reactions" by Kurt Lang and Gladys Engel Lang, *Public Opinion Quarterly*, Vol. XXV (Summer 1961), pp. 277–288. Reprinted by permission.

PART 1: 1940

Roger Morton managed a prosperous insurance business in the quiet northern Ohio town where he had lived since boyhood. Forty-five years old, he was married, the father of two children, a regular attendant at the local Congregational Church, a leading figure in the Rotary Club, and a lifelong member of the Republican Party.

Thus, as the spring of 1940 arrived and, with it, talk of the forthcoming presidential election, Roger had no trouble in making up his mind. He knew who the Democratic candidate would be. Franklin D. Roosevelt would certainly obtain his party's endorsement for another term. Rather than see "that man" in the White House for the third time, Roger was prepared to vote for anyone the opposition put up.

Personally, he preferred to see the nomination go to Senator Robert Taft, a native Ohioan. However, when the little-known Wendell Willkie was acclaimed in July as the GOP's candidate, Roger was quite pleased. He believed Willkie's rags-to-riches career would appeal to the American public. Indeed, it would perhaps contrast favorably with F.D.R.'s patrician background.

Roger detested Roosevelt. He was indignant at the government's growing interference in business. He scorned federal projects, such as the WPA (Works Projects Administration) and other schemes which "coddled the unemployed and lazy." He was uneasy about the soaring national debt produced by the New Deal's many projects. And he felt certain the President was leading the country into a European war that was "none of America's business." Above all, the idea of a third term made him furious.

Roger took an active interest in the campaign from the beginning. He kept informed on the issues by reading and listening to the radio commentators, and he attempted to persuade prospective voters who were not completely sure. He was positive his choice was the right one, and his opinions were continuously bolstered by the vast majority of people he came across. They felt exactly as he did.

Charlie O'Neill, in contrast, took little interest in the campaign. He did not reach a final decision until November 1—just

CROWD AND MASS BEHAVIOR

four days before the election. At 28, he was an up-and-coming accountant in the city of Sandusky, Ohio, to which his Irish grandfather had immigrated at the turn of the century. A bachelor and a Catholic who had had two years in business college, he was chiefly concerned with staying employed and getting ahead in the world.

Charlie had voted for Roosevelt in 1936, a natural enough choice in a family of registered Democrats. But Charlie did not always see eye-to-eye with the members of his family. They were, after all, a bit old-fashioned and not very well educated. He thought vaguely that it probably *was* time for a change in 1940, that a third term was not a good precedent in American politics. But his views were not definite enough to risk rocking the boat at home.

When, in July, Wendell Willkie, an unknown, a "dark horse," emerged as the Republican nominee, Charlie was genuinely impressed. He admired Willkie as a self-made man and he believed that business experience would be an asset to a President, especially at a time when business was bad, as it had been for the past ten years. His boss and many of his coworkers felt this way, too, and early became enthusiastic boosters of the candidate from Indiana. Therefore, throughout the summer Charlie leaned in this direction.

Nevertheless, he was a bit resentful whenever he heard old-line Republicans talking about "WPA freeloaders," unemployed "shirkers," and "union bums." His own father had lost his job in 1934 and had never found another. Charlie's younger brother, who worked in a factory, had persuaded Charlie that unions were the only protector of the working class. The Republican line of talk just made Charlie want to forget about politics altogether.

The Battle of Britain which raged throughout August and September of that year added to his confusion. As an Irishman, he had never felt any love for the English; yet he found himself rooting for them. He was glad an experienced leader like Roosevelt was at the helm during such times. However, he opposed the draft, which the President had recently introduced. And Willkie promised to keep America out of the war.

By October, Charlie believed that the outcome of the election would not make much difference because both candidates had positive merits. He even considered not voting at all. However, at the eleventh hour, he made a decision—in favor of Roosevelt—not as the result of weighing all the pros and cons but simply as the result of something emotional his father had said about "the little people of the country depending on F.D.R."

Roger Morton's ability to make up his mind very early in the campaign and Charlie O'Neill's inability to come to a decision until the last minute illustrate a pattern that three sociologists of Columbia University, Paul F. Lazarsfeld, Bernard Berelson, and Hazel Gaudet, found to be typical in 1940. Their findings indicate that the *time* of a voter's final decision is influenced by two conditions—the strength of his interest in the election and the number of cross-pressures operating on him.

To find out how voters actually reached their decisions, the research team conducted the first scientific survey of voting. In May of 1940 they picked 3000 people in Erie County, Ohio, an area which usually voted in the same way as the whole nation. The 3000 were selected as representative of the population of the county as a whole. They further selected 600 persons who were then interviewed seven times during the course of the election period, or once every month from May through November. In this way, they discovered how individuals responded to the campaign propaganda as well as how they were influenced by certain socioeconomic or family factors. This is what they found:

Voters fell into three categories: "May Voters"—those who knew prior to the campaign how they would vote and maintained their choice throughout the election period; "June-to-August Voters"—those who settled upon a candidate during the convention period; and "September-to-November Voters"—those who did not definitely make up their minds until the last few months, weeks, or even days of the campaign.

Generally speaking, the sociologists found that the people who delayed deciding took less interest in the election than the others did. Further, those who made their choice late in the campaign were subject to more cross-pressures: there were more conflicts and inconsistencies among the factors which influenced their final decisions. And the cross-pressures pulled these voters in opposite directions so that a choice was made very difficult.

CROWD AND MASS BEHAVIOR

INTEREST AND TIME OF DECISION

The more interested that people were in the election, the sooner they decided definitely how they would vote. For instance, almost two-thirds (63 percent) of those greatly interested had already made up their minds by May. But only 41 percent of the voters with less interest in the election had made up their minds so early. Looking at it from the other end of the interval, only 12 percent of the greatly interested waited until September or later before finally deciding how to vote, whereas twice as high a proportion (25 percent) of the less interested delayed their decision until then.

Early deciders also tended to be "very anxious" to see their candidate elected, while those who picked their man during the summer or the fall tended to feel, respectively, that the election was "not terribly important" or that it "made no difference." In fact, 66 percent of the respondents who felt that the election made no difference waited until the September–November period to make up their minds. To the campaign managers, this meant they had to propagandize a steadily shrinking segment of the electorate (those who remained undecided), a segment whose interest in the election was continually lessening.

CROSS-PRESSURES AND TIME OF DECISION

Roger Morton, as we have seen, was completely free of cross-pressures. Roger felt no need to weigh various factors in coming to a decision. Following the campaign closely served only to confirm his original choice. Charlie O'Neill, on the other hand, was beset from the beginning by a multitude of opposing influences.

In 1940 the following cross-pressures could affect a voter's time of decision:

1. *Religion and Socioeconomic Status.* Traditionally, Protestants have been identified with the Republican Party, while Catholics have more often identified with the Democratic Party. In addition, individuals of higher socioeconomic status tend to vote Republican and people of lower socioeconomic status are more likely to vote Democratic. It is also true that Protestants as a group have attained a higher socioeconomic level in the United States than have Catholics. Cross-pressure would be felt, then, by an individual if he were both Catholic *and* prosperous

or both Protestant *and* poor. Charlie O'Neill was subject to this particular cross-pressure. He was Catholic but he also enjoyed a good income for a man of his age and had excellent prospects for the future.

2. Occupational Identification. Participants in the survey were asked to give their occupations and also to state with what group in the community they identified themselves: big business, small business, labor, farming, and so on. Ordinarily, an individual's occupation determines his feeling of identification. However, sometimes an unskilled worker thinks of himself as belonging with the business class, while a white-collar employee thinks he belongs with labor. Since business usually supports the Republican Party and labor votes for the Democratic Party, a cross-pressure would be present if a voter's actual occupation conflicted with his idea of where he belonged. Charlie O'Neill was caught in this dilemma, too. As an accountant, he "should have" identified himself with business. But in actuality he was very conscious of his family's origins and of the fact that his father and brother were "working people." Therefore, his "instinctive" identification was with labor.

3. The 1936 Vote and the 1940 Vote. Most people in the survey voted for the same party in both presidential elections. Those who changed parties between 1936 and 1940 had to overcome a psychological hurdle which could be considered a cross-pressure. Some, like Charlie, could not quite make the leap.

4. The Voter and His Family. The typical American family exhibits considerable political solidarity, with all adult members voting the same way. But where members of a voter's family disagree with him or are undecided, a cross-pressure is created which makes a definite decision harder to reach. Charlie was confused by this, too.

5. The Voter and His Associates. Friends, like one's family, can create a political environment, either congenial or hostile. Republicans who felt the country was swinging toward Willkie (as did Roger Morton) and Democrats who thought the tide was turning toward Roosevelt found it easy to decide how to vote, because their environment reinforced their preferences. However, those who were aware of some people swinging to Willkie and others to Roosevelt were subject to conflicting pressures.

6. *1940 Voting Intention and Attitude Toward Business and Government.* A person's voting intention may contradict his attitude on a basic issue of the election. For instance, in 1940, most people who intended to vote Republican wanted a President with business experience, while most people who expected to vote Democratic preferred a candidate with experience in government. However, there were some Republicans who felt government experience was of higher value in a candidate and some Democrats, like Charlie, who thought business experience was a more important qualification. Individuals in such situations as these were naturally subject to cross-pressures.

The more evenly balanced the opposing pressures were, the longer the voter delayed making up his mind. This was chiefly because, as with Charlie O'Neill, such a voter had good reason to vote for either of the candidates.

Interest and Cross-Pressures

How are interest and cross-pressures related? Controversy makes issues exciting. Those individuals who had the greatest difficulty making a decision might have been the very ones most involved in the campaign. However, this is not the way most individuals adjust to conflict-ridden situations. Often, when people desire and shun a course of action in almost equal degree, they do not decide either for *or* against it. Instead, they may change the subject or avoid the problem altogether.

Thus many voters subject to cross-pressures tended to belittle the whole affair. Like Charlie, they avoided real conflict by losing interest in the election. They had no clear-cut stake in the victory of either candidate. On the other hand, those under no cross-pressures showed most interest in the election. But even one cross-pressure meant a substantial decrease in the voters' interest. For example, among those who were under no cross-pressures, 44 percent expressed great interest in the election. Among those who felt one cross-pressure the proportion greatly interested was 31 percent, and among those who suffered from several cross-pressures the proportion greatly interested was only 27 percent.

How do both factors—number of cross-pressures and degree of interest—work jointly to affect the time of final decision?

Understandably, people who are subjected to no or only one

cross-pressure and who take great interest in the election make up their minds first. Fully 73 percent of them knew in May how they would vote in November, while only seven percent in this category waited until the final period. At the other extreme were those who felt two or more cross-pressures and who did not show much interest in the election: Only 26 percent of them decided as early as May, while 33 percent waited until the last weeks of the campaign to make up their minds between Roosevelt, the Democratic candidate, and Willkie, the Republican candidate.

CHANGERS AND TIME OF FINAL DECISION

Lazarsfeld, Berelson, and Gaudet classified the people who did not make up their minds until some time during the campaign proper (here called "changers") in three main categories: *crystallizers*, or those who were not fully aware of a voting intention in May yet who, because of their position in the social structure, were disposed all along to vote in a certain way and as the campaign went on, their attitude came out in the open; *waverers*, or those who started out with a definite intention, later fell away from it (either to "don't know" or to the other party), but eventually returned to their original choice; and *party changers*, or those who originally intended to vote for one party but later went over to the camp of the opposition and stayed there.

Was it easier for certain kinds of changers to reach a final decision than it was for others? Apparently, it was: 68 percent of the crystallizers were able to settle their vote by August (following both conventions), as against only 48 percent of the party changers and 46 percent of the waverers.

Not surprisingly, the vacillators are the target of the politicians' efforts in the last stages of a presidential campaign. The Charlies of this world, in fact, are the people who swing elections. The irony is that they are the ones least responsive to the professionals' propaganda. Like Charlie, they are much more likely to be influenced by the person who "got to them" last before Election Day. Thus the notion that the people who switch parties during the campaign are mainly reasoning, thoughtful, conscientious people who are convinced by the issues is wrong; Lazarsfeld, Berelson, and Gaudet found that they are usually just the opposite.

PART 2: 1960

Twenty years later, Roger Morton, now retired and still Republican, shared with a now older but still politically uncertain Charlie O'Neill a new influence—television. While there can be little doubt that John Kennedy's narrow victory came from a variety of complicated factors, the vibrant, attractive young Senator projected an image into millions of American living rooms which affected the decision of many voters. How significant was this new means of communication in the business of politics?

During the campaign of 1960, John Kennedy and Richard Nixon, the two presidential candidates, debated against each other on national television on four occasions. Kurt and Gladys Lang, two sociologists from Queens College in New York, had already decided to investigate just how the voters would respond to the twin assault of the debaters. Would a substantial portion of the voters be swayed? Participating in their study were 95 New York viewers, of whom some were potential Kennedy supporters and others were potential Nixon supporters. To measure their reactions, each of the respondents was interviewed three times: late in September, just before the first debate; again, immediately after that debate; and finally, after the fourth and last encounter between the antagonists.

Kennedy picked up most of the undecided voters among the respondents. Of the 23 persons who were undecided in the beginning, 15 had either decided for Kennedy or were clearly leaning toward him by the end of the fourth debate. But only three had moved into the Nixon column. Five were still undecided or determined not to vote. The undecided voters shifted decisively immediately after the first debate. At that time eight of the uncommitted decided on Kennedy and four more showed pro-Kennedy leanings.

In addition, four persons who were "definitely" committed before the debates switched from one candidate to the other—three from Nixon to Kennedy, one from Kennedy to Nixon. But while the pro-Kennedy switch occurred immediately after the first debate, the pro-Nixon switch did not seem to be related in any way to that first television encounter.

Altogether, there were 22 changes of vote during the course

of the campaign, of which 18 were "crystallizers" (from an un-decided position) and four were switchers (from one candidate to the other). Kennedy drew his added strength largely (11 out of 18) from voters who could be considered Democrats but who nevertheless felt only weakly identified with the Democratic Party. And Nixon picked up just four votes, capturing three Dem-ocrats and an Independent. Therefore, very few of the shifts at-tributed to the debates were actually contrary to past political commitments. The majority apparently were acting on inclina-tions which had not been changed by the debates. All the same, the debates brought about a sharper polarization in the voters' attitudes. This happened primarily because of the images the candidates projected on television.

How the Images of Nixon and Kennedy Changed

Before the debates, 70 percent of the respondents were "more familiar" with Nixon; only 12 percent knew Kennedy bet-ter. Yet certain well-defined images of the two candidates were widely shared by the members of the panel no matter where they stood politically.

Nixon, who had been Vice-President under Eisenhower, was generally believed to be better prepared for the Presidency than was Kennedy, the senator. Nixon was remembered as a roving ambassador who had faced angry mobs in South America and had debated against Khrushchev in Russia. An experienced poli-tician, he was expected to be a formidable TV opponent.

Although considered a competent political organizer and a vigorous personality, Kennedy was widely believed to be too im-mature and inexperienced for the Presidency. Many accused him of being overambitious, insincere, or snobbish, while others sus-pected that his family or religion might exert improper influence upon his conduct in office.

As they prepared to watch the first Nixon-Kennedy debate, both Roger and Charlie were in approximately the same state of mind they had been in shortly before the election in 1940. Roger shared the confidence of two-thirds of Nixon's supporters that their candidate was a superior debater, while Charlie and only about one-third of Kennedy's partisans believed that their man would be a match for the Vice-President.

All this changed dramatically after the first debate. In fact, 89 percent of those who watched the opening television encounter thought Kennedy had either bested Nixon or had fought him to a draw. Thus, as a result of this single debate, Richard Nixon's image as a champion debater and expert television politician was destroyed. This helped crystallize the votes of the undecided and forced those who had made their choice to revise their estimates of the candidates.

Forty-five percent of the respondents gained an improved overall impression of Kennedy after the first debate, while only ten percent reached a better impression of Nixon. More to the point, 22 percent reported that their evaluation of Nixon had gone down in contrast to one percent who reported that their image of Kennedy had deteriorated.

Prejudice Outwits TV

After the first debate, the respondents' images of the candidates changed very little during the remainder of the campaign. Yet many viewers, especially Nixon supporters, had received impressions of the candidates that ran counter to their basic political preferences. But the improvement in Kennedy's image and the deterioration in Nixon's image were not accompanied by any significant shift in voting intentions among those previously committed to Nixon. The viewers overcame these jarring impressions and maintained or regained confidence in their original choice.

Nixon supporters responded to the strain produced by their favorite's poor TV performance in several ways. Some belittled debating and performing skills. Others focused on the policies advocated by Nixon with which they already agreed and ignored his failure to "put over" these policies in verbal competition. Still others imputed to Kennedy unfavorable personal traits on the basis of certain television mannerisms which they could quite as well have interpreted in a positive light. Kennedy partisans, of course, employed the same psychological techniques to support *their* particular biases. The difference was that their candidate's good showing in the debates prevented TV from acting as a cross-pressure as it did in the case of the Nixon followers.

The conclusion from the study of the debates is that while television can produce some dramatic changes in a candidate's image, its effect on the voters' final choice is limited. Voters with already strong commitments simply adjust the TV images to their old preferences. In short, Kennedy's television "triumph" had its greatest effect on people who would probably have voted Democratic anyway.

The primary effect of television exposure, then, was to crystallize the political decisions of the uncommitted at an earlier point in the campaign than might have been expected in, for example, the election of 1940. But the Langs point to some possible indirect "sleeper" effects not covered by their research. One such effect is the long-range influence of lasting impressions of the two candidates and their performance in the debates. Thus they suggest that TV, by projecting a favorable image of Kennedy and showing Nixon in an unfavorable light, probably heartened Kennedy's campaign workers and inspired them to greater effort.

The Peace Marchers*

What kinds of people took part in the Peace March of 1968?

What influenced them to join it?

Which is the most effective influence on an individual's decision to march: the mass media, membership in an antiwar organization, or informal personal contacts?

Did the marchers have a specific complaint, or were they protesting against general conditions of social life such as crime and poverty?

What sort of individuals expected violence during the March?

On Friday, October 25, 1968, Edward Forsyth and Sarah Topping were eating lunch on a campus near London.

Sarah asked, "Well, do we march Sunday or not?"

Edward looked thoughtful. "I think so. I've decided that I owe it to my lofty principles. And to our future children."

Both laughed. They planned to be married in June.

"But I don't know about you. I don't want you to get beaten or gassed."

"Edward, you silly goose, I can take care of myself. Besides, it may be more peaceful than you think. Let's go."

Thus, two people decided to march in the Vietnam Peace March, held in London, England, on October 27, 1968. Some 50,000 others marched, too, and the demonstration received extensive attention in mass media all over the world.

Why did they march? This was the question that puzzled Paul Barker, editor of *New Society*, a British weekly that features

---

* Adapted from "Portrait of a Protest" by Paul Barker, Humphrey Taylor, Emanuel de Kadt, and Earl Hopper, *New Society*, Vol. XII (October 31, 1968), pp. 631–634. This article first appeared in *New Society*, the weekly review of the social sciences, 128 Long Acre, London W.C.2. England. Reprinted by permission.

news of interest to social scientists. After considerable discussion he and his colleagues, Humphrey Taylor (of the Opinion Research Centre) and Emanuel de Kadt and Earl Hopper (two sociologists from the London School of Economics), decided to conduct interviews with a sample of the marchers—in the very act of marching.

Consequently, on Sunday a team of 15 interviewers appeared among the demonstrators. They interviewed only persons who said they supported the March—to rule out spectators. By dusk they had 270 usable interviews, which they considered a fair sample of the participants. The social class of the respondents was determined by asking their occupation (either "manual" or "nonmanual"). In the case of students, the occupation of the father was taken as an indicator of their social class.

The findings provide greater insight into the motivation of the marchers than can be found in newspaper accounts. Moreover, they have a special kind of validity because the replies were gathered "on the wing." They lack the bias which faulty memory may introduce when interviews are done some time after the event. The findings of this research supply revealing materials for the study of collective incidents, such as the Peace March, when thousands of persons somehow come together to do a certain thing, but without organized planning.

Why did these people march? The answer to this question is what the survey sought to find out. In seeking the answer, the investigators asked three questions: (1) What kind of people were the marchers? (2) What outside influences worked on them? (3) What were their beliefs about war and political affairs?

1. Who were they? The marchers were for the most part young male students. Some came from families of the working class. But most had parents of the middle class. Four out of five were male, and only one-fourth were 25 years of age or older. Almost half were university-trained. Seven out of ten had taken part in earlier political demonstrations.

2. What brought them to the March? The mass media did not appear as influential as might be expected. Only three percent credited television with bringing them out; three percent more mentioned wall posters or slogans as the stimulus; and 13 percent said the newspapers had had the most influence on their decision. If mass communication was not considered crucial, informal communication was. Well over half said other people had influenced them to march—28 percent pointed to a political group they belonged to, and 29 percent just said "friends." (The rest gave miscellaneous replies.)

3. *What were their beliefs?* The first of three questions on beliefs asked the marchers to name the focus of their protest. In response to the interviewer's check list, most people named several targets of their feelings, namely:

U.S. policy in Vietnam	96%
U.S. policies in general	69
British policy on Vietnam	85
The general structure of British society	65
Capitalism in general	68
All forms of authority	23
Other	10

The second question on attitudes probed whether the individual hoped for a victory for the Vietcong or a compromise end to the war. Fully 53 percent said they wanted a victory for the Vietcong, as against 42 percent who preferred a compromise. The remaining five percent had no opinion.

The third question dealt more with actions than beliefs. The interviewers asked, "Have you ever belonged to, or actively supported, any of the following?" When tallied, the past allegiances of the marchers proved to be:

Conservative party	4%
Liberal party	5
Labour party	28
Communists	24
Anarchists	11
Committee for Nuclear Disarmament	44
Committee of 100	24
Revolutionary Socialist Students Federation	20
Any other socialist groups	17

Finally, the survey asked if the respondent expected violence during the March, and if he personally expected to be involved in violence. While 70 percent expected violence, only ten percent of the respondents anticipated that they would be embroiled in it.

In summary: The answers show that many marchers held fairly radical views and were discontent with domestic and international conditions. Most hoped for changes in social institutions. Yet the question remained: Would such a dissenting aggregation of persons resort to violence? Would the 70 percent who thought so prove to be correct?

Political orientations differed, of course, between subportions of the demonstrators. The biggest contrast was found between students of working-class background and all the rest. The former group was more anticapitalist (86 percent), and more in favor of a victory for the Vietcong (69 percent). More of them (80 percent) expected violence. On the other hand, they had the lowest proportion supporting the Labour party—only 20 percent. Ironically, because of their extended education, the same young people would win better jobs within the system and would have to face the tension of deciding between joining or rejecting "the Establishment."

Age, oddly enough, did not produce big differences. Little "generation gap" * appeared in political attitudes. It must be kept in mind, however, that the older marchers were not representative of their age group in British society.

What the observer saw—for most of the day—was a parade of all kinds of people, often animated and gay, striding through the streets. Some walked alone, others were in pairs, and some marched with a group—perhaps from a neighborhood or a school or factory. Many carried banners: "No More War"; "Yankee Go Home"; "Workers for Peace"; "Defeat U.S. Imperialism"; "Notting Hill Red Guard"; "Victory to the NLF"; "Support Greek Resistance"; "West Ham Anarchists." Posters pictured their heroes: Ho Chi-Minh, Che Guevara, Gandhi, Lenin, even one of the Beatles—John Lennon. A large contingent from the London School of Economics chanted "Ho, Ho, Ho Chi-Minh." Others sang, "All we are saying is give peace a chance."

But the style and atmosphere were far from grim. A news-

---

* See "Whose Generation Gap?" in this book.

CROWD AND MASS BEHAVIOR

paper noted: "It was more of a picnic than a revolution. These young people are more interested in making love than in making war." A radical union leader growled, "These kids are more adventurous than serious; they don't have the discipline needed for industrial activity." Another commentator pointed out that the chant of "Ho, Ho, Ho Chi-Minh" was more like a U.S. cheerleader's rally than a call to revolution.

The procession moved along the Thames to Trafalgar Square, along Whitehall to Parliament Square and finally to Hyde Park for speeches. Edward and Sarah were joined by two young men of about their age, George and Stub, who worked in a warehouse near the docks in East London, and were out to "show the bigwigs what's what," as George put it. Neither of them had been to the University, but the four got along well, perhaps because they agreed on the waste and destruction wrought by the war in Vietnam. When Sarah asked why they had decided to join the March, George, who seemed to be the spokesman for the pair, said, "We usually just fool around on Sunday, or play football (soccer). But some of the chaps at the plant were talking about the March last week, and when Stub and I heard it on the telly (TV) this morning we decided to come along. Besides, my father was killed fighting in Malaysia, so I'm not really keen on wars of any kind. I was so young I never even knew him."

As they headed up the street away from the Thames, a man with a clipboard came up to Edward, introduced himself as a pollster and requested an interview. Edward was happy to agree.

When the interviewer left, George wanted to know what the talk was all about. Having taken sociology and political science courses, Edward explained opinion surveys to the others: "Scholars and writers have been asking people how they felt about things for a long time—probably as far back as Herodotus and Thucydides in Athens of the fifth century, B.C. In France, about 150 years ago, a man named Le Play did lots of interviewing about how families spent their money. Polls really got their start in the States in 1935 with Dr. Gallup."

For the first time, Stub showed an interest in the conversation. "What do they do with all the answers?" he asked.

George told him how the pollsters tallied the responses into categories like "agree" and "disagree" and then published them in the newspapers, or broadcast them on the wireless (radio) and telly (TV).

"They're very influential," Sarah said. "The Prime Minister and Parliament really pay attention when the polls come out to find out how the people feel about an issue."

Stub was not impressed. "They never ask me any questions, or anybody down where I live. I've never even heard of them before."

Edward, the social science student, was ready for this one. He told them about sampling. "They draw a sample by scientific means, to be representative of the population they're studying. In the States, for example, Gallup and Harris do only 1500 interviews for the entire country, and their results are usually—although not always—very close to the final totals.

Sarah was an art major. Although she had studied sociology, she did not completely understand sampling either. "How do you suppose they drew a sample of this mob?"

Edward had to admit he did not know. "Usually they do the interviews at homes, and draw their sample from census statistics. That's not too difficult. But here, I believe, they station interviewers at different sections of the parade, and each one tries to pick people at random, so that they will somehow get a representative sample of all of us."

Edward was not too far off. Barker and his colleagues had indeed followed this general plan. They believed that they had obtained a fair sample, although they could not guarantee that it was as representative as those samples gained in house-to-house surveys.

The talk turned to the questions themselves. George was puzzled by the groups the interviewer had asked about.

"I've never met anybody who was a Conservative, or a member of the Liberal party," he said. "All I know are people from the Labour party, and some Communists."

"I've got to admit," Edward said, "that we've got plenty of groups in this country. Most people don't know very much about them, except the two big ones—Conservative and Labour. Since the bomb and Vietnam, lots of people have grown angry enough to start sounding off about how they feel. That's one thing about England—we've always had people who would stand up and say they disagreed with what was going on. Some people even favored the Thirteen Colonies back in 1776."

"Stub and I never finished school," said George. "You're really up on things."

Edward told them that he and Sarah were in college and that he wanted to be a teacher.

"One group that is pretty new," Sarah added, "is the anarchists. We have some at college. I can't quite figure them out, except that they seem to be against everything. One girl in my class works with them. She's OK, but she keeps saying the same things over and over."

Edward spoke up again. "I know some anarchists, too. I agree with most of their criticisms, but I can't see that they have much else to offer. They argue that the world today is in such bad shape that things must be changed—somehow, and fast. When I ask them for a program or a blueprint, they always say the French revolutionaries did not have a program in 1789, and *they* came out pretty well."

Said George, "We have some fellows at the plant who talk like that, only I didn't know they were anarchists. They're just chaps who are always saying that all we have to do is look around us, and we will know that things are not so good. Wars, and crime, and the bomb, and the politicians, and people going hungry. You know, maybe I'm an anarchist, too."

They all smiled.

"Maybe" said Edward, "but I doubt it. On the poll the anarchists would have said they were against all forms of authority. And they would have expected violence today, and would have expected to be in the midst of the violence themselves. I'm not really clear about anarchists either, but so far I don't think you are one."

As has been mentioned, 23 percent of the respondents said they were protesting all forms of authority; ten percent said they expected to be involved in violence; and 11 percent said they had belonged to, or supported the anarchists. Even though these figures may appear fairly high, the role of the anarchists in the protest movement had been overrated. Most of the 11 percent, the pollsters thought, were not true anarchists, but people in various stages of alienation from society. Certainly anarchists had been active in the preparations, and some had talked of dynamite, but this hard core produced no explosions during the March.

Actually, the London Peace March was more organized than the research team indicated. It seems true that many, probably most, of the marchers made individual decisions to join the demonstration. Or they came with friends, like Edward and Sarah and George and Stub. They were individuals making up a "mass" —each had individually decided to do the same thing at the same time and place but inspired by a common cause.

A reading of the newspapers, however, provides a different perspective, one of organized, planned activity. The largest organization was the Vietnam Solidarity Campaign (VSC), whose 26 satellite groups helped with the arrangements. Splitting off from the VSC was a smaller but more militant group called the Maoist-British Vietnam Solidarity Front.

The Front had disagreed with the VSC's plans. Its leaders believed that a peaceful demonstration was not enough, that conditions warranted more extreme means. It is not surprising, then, that the day's chief violence was the Front's attack on the American Embassy in Grosvenor Square.

Their charge was well planned, but Scotland Yard had been tipped off and had 1000 uniformed men guarding the Embassy. They stood their ground as several thousand demonstrators, according to the *London Times*, "charged like a rugby scrum in arrowhead form." (The *New York Times* said they rushed in "a flying wedge, heads down and arms linked.") They were not strong enough, however, to break through the police lines, which reflect the police training and discipline.

Furious at their defeat, the militants began shouting at the bystanders—many of them marchers but committed to nonviolence. "What's wrong, got weak knees?" "Why did you come, to see a Western?" "If you don't believe in violence, why did you come?" Almost no members of the VSC, apparently, took part in the rushing.

At these taunts, George asked Stub, "Shall we have a go at the coppers?"

"Not me!" snapped Stub. "I'm wearing my new suit and still owe 30 bob on it."

Edward couldn't resist a jibe. "Fine pair of anarchists you are!"

The day's only violence, then, was a planned event, but as it happened, it proved to be a defeat for the extremists. Almost everyone—even the official Communist newspaper in London—praised the police for their restraint as well as for their effectiveness. The *New York Times* reported that the officers never drew their truncheons and never showed anger.

All in all, the March pleased most observers. The *London Times* editorialized: "The events of yesterday justify a feeling of pride and confidence that free democracy is of mature and hardy growth in Britain."

The Flowering of the
Hippie Movement*

What set of motives led young people to be attracted to the hippie phenomenon?

What relationship did the hippie phenomenon have to earlier youth and bohemian movements?

What accounted for the collapse of the Haight-Ashbury experiment in a new life style?

"Everyone came to listen to the music," said Joe a week later, recalling the rock music festival at Woodstock. "Nobody knew everybody was going to be up there and feel all together and have that feeling. It was the same thing at the peace march in Chicago. You'd pass someone young or someone with long hair and you'd smile at each other. Or you'd give each other the peace sign, or know that he was thinking the same way you were thinking. And like the blacks go by each other and say 'brother.'"

"I saw one instance where a fight could have broken out very easily," Ben broke in. "But the people who were going to fight were in the midst of 300,000 people, all talking about love and happiness and they couldn't do it. You knew the others thought quite a bit like you did. And you knew you weren't out against the world."

"We shared everything," Ted said. "We went to sleep, just the two of us, under one canopy. When I woke up, there were a dozen people under it with us and we all stayed together for the rest of the time up there at Woodstock. We shared food, too."

"Like Saturday," put in Marge. "We were sitting there and

* Adapted from "The Flowering of the Hippie Movement" by John Robert Howard, *The Annals* (Philadelphia: The American Academy of Political and Social Science), Vol. 382 (March 1969), pp. 43–55. Reprinted by permission.

this watermelon came by with three mouthfuls taken out of it. You were supposed to take a bite and pass it on. Because some guy three rows over said, 'Give those people some watermelon.'"

These four speakers had been part of the crowd at Woodstock. Between August 15 and 17, 1969, at least 300,000 young people—some newspapers said it was 400,000—had converged on the tiny Catskills village of Bethel, near Woodstock, New York, to take part in what was billed as the most ambitious rock music festival ever held. But what happened there appeared more like a mass movement.

What went on over that long weekend? The supply of food ran out. So did drinking water. Garbage and refuse piled up. Rain turned the ground to mud. Everyone was wet and hungry. And there were no security forces of any official nature inside the camp grounds to control the assembled thousands. The news broadcasts mentioned "bad trips" on drugs and the possibility of epidemics and riots. The potential for violence and catastrophe was enormous.

Surprisingly, the expected disaster never materialized. People sang, danced, swam in the nearby ponds in intervals when the sun shone, read quietly among the sprawling bodies, and communed with nature and each other. The smoke and the sweetish odor of "pot" hung in the air: it was estimated that over 90 percent were smoking marijuana. Food was shared freely and casually. Still more food was flown in by helicopter. The sick were given sympathy and help; so were the "freaked out" and "tripped up." Order and good humor prevailed through the whole weekend in the hippie spirit of love, tolerance, and nonviolence.

When the end of the weekend and the merciless rain brought the festival to a close, many who had made the pilgrimage had heard no music at all. Over 4,000 had not even gotten into the festival grounds, locked in a traffic jam that clogged the roads for a radius of eight miles. But amidst the chaos they had found "community" and they stayed on because it was "groovy." The presence of other young people was a powerful magnet. No one knows how many there were true hippies, but the hippie creed of love and human sympathy seemed to infect them all. As they would say, there were good "vibes" (vibrations). Again and again the newspaper reporters interviewing at the site were told of the thrill, the glow of friendly feeling, and the sentiment of communion which enhanced the whole weekend.

Adults were appalled that drugs had been openly hawked and used at the festival. But on the other hand, they were impressed by the fact that a throng of young people, as large as the population of Rochester, New York, had kept its "cool."

Furthermore, the reports of the young people's courteousness, cooperativeness, and good behavior in general shocked many critics into a revision of their previously hostile attitudes. Surely, such a generation of young people could not be all bad!

John Robert Howard, a sociologist at the City College of New York, saw in Woodstock a happening of great significance for what it reveals of the attitudes of young people today. He sought to discover who, exactly, are the hippies. What are the special characteristics of their movement? And what impact are they having on society at large? In the research presented here Howard begins his analysis with a brief history of the hippie movement.

The hippies were first noticed in San Francisco some time in the mid-sixties in the wake of the cultural explosion associated with rock music. The Haight-Ashbury section of the city was their domain. By the summer of 1967 both the "flower children" and their cultural capital were household words throughout America. They also proved powerful attractions to large numbers of the country's youth, who came to Haight-Ashbury square by motorcycle or battered flower-speckled car or as hitchhikers. Hippies of one kind or another began appearing so fast that soon it was impossible to know just who or what the name meant. John Howard distinguished four types of character commonly found on the hippie scene: the visionaries, the "freaks" and "heads," the plastic hippies, and the midnight hippies.

THE VISIONARIES

The visionaries gave birth to the movement. Their criticism of American life went deep, extending to all aspects of the social system. But unlike liberal critics, who try to reform the system from within, the visionaries wanted no part in it at all. And unlike

102

revolutionaries of the type who hope to gain power in order to effect radical change, the hippies hoped to transform society by the example they set others. What they asked was simply the freedom to "do their thing," in other words, to create their own social system and live in it.

These early hippies believed that life should be gentler, less competitive, more tolerant and that there should be no separation of mind and body. The worship of "things," to their way of thinking, destroys human values in modern industrial societies. Thus people are needlessly cut off from one another. But their chief complaint was that the rewards in society are in terms of money and a certain standard of living but the work roles and occupations which yield the income and the standard of living are, for the most part, if not degrading at least meaningless. Furthermore, the hippies insisted that the material goods that make up the high standard of living—the split-level ranch house in the suburbs, the swimming pool, the color television set, and all the other possessions that are so insistently advertised—are unsatisfying. The American tragedy, as they see it, is that the "normal" American judges himself and others according to these dehumanizing standards.

In opposition, the hippies turned traditional values upside down. Instead of making "good" use of their time, they "wasted" it. Instead of striving to get ahead, they lived in voluntary poverty. The character of their experiment can be illustrated by certain of their actions which many observers found shocking.

For one thing: a hippie group called the Diggers began feeding people free in the parks of San Francisco and Berkeley. They had begged for the food. They refused to accept the idea that the right of people to eat should depend on money. Instead, the Diggers tried to relate to other people in terms of their needs. They opened free stores, where anyone could come and take what he needed. They rented apartments ("pads") in readiness for the weary teenaged dropouts * who made their way to San Francisco. Some of the rock groups gave free concerts in the park.

The hippies rejected conventional society with its power

* See "The High School Dropout" in *Life in Families* in this *Readings in Sociology* Series.

structure and its values—"the Establishment" as its critics call it. For example, they argued that the main purpose of the school system, particularly at the college level, is to prepare people for certain occupational roles. However, if one does not want the money and the type of life such an occupation affords, then there is no point in preparing for it. Anyone who drops out is then free to live in his own way. This might be anything, from making sandals or pottery or reed pipes, to exploring various levels of consciousness, to working the soil as a farmer and grinding one's own wheat for bread.

In short, the hippies were true revolutionaries, despairing of this world and fixing their hopes on a new and, they thought, better world. They had a vision of people "grooving" together, communing and sharing, as they did later on at Woodstock. They tried to abolish property rights, race prejudice, and conventional conceptions of what is moral or immoral and all other barriers to achieving a sense of community. They assumed that all essential needs can be satisfied if everyone does what he wants to do, of his own free will. They believed that this goal can be achieved without the use of authority or any kind of power. In their own way of life the early "hippies" demonstrated their ideal of society.

The original San Francisco group of hippies split up by the summer of 1968.* For one thing, the police harassed them. Moreover, their organization was loose and weak, for, strictly speaking, they were still a movement—the phase of organization came later. No one had the authority to give orders. A Digger told Howard why, for example, he and his fellow hippies had stopped passing out free food in the park.

> Well, man, it took a lot of organization to get that done. We had to scuffle to get the food. Then the chicks or somebody had to prepare it. Then we got to serve it. A lot of people got to do a lot of things at the right time or it doesn't come off. Well, it got so that people weren't doing it. I mean a cat wouldn't let us have his truck when we needed it or some chick is grooving somewhere and can't help out. Now you hate to get into a power bag and start telling people what to do. But without that, man, well!

* See "Two Social Movements and Their Fates" in this book.

Many of the Diggers and others have moved to the hills of California and other western states to set up rural communes. There they hope to establish an orderly system within which, together, they may put their beliefs into practice. And they founded urban communes, as well, in many eastern cities. The communal households pooled their resources (some of the members were able to get jobs) and tried to save one another from the compromising necessity of asking their parents for money.

FREAKS AND HEADS

The visionaries use drugs, but drugs are not fundamental to their way of life. However, there are other hippies who use drugs extensively. The most commonly used drugs are marijuana and hashish, which are derived from plants, and LSD and methedrine ("speed"), which are manufactured from chemicals.*

The smoking of marijuana, the mildest and most popular of the drugs, became so widespread among youth by the late 1960s that its users probably include many who do not fit into the hippie category. Some smoke it simply as a way of being "in" or "with it." Others find it produces a mild euphoria (feeling of well being). But to still others, "turning on" is an important part of daily life and heavy users, called "pot heads," are closely identified with the hippies and their haunts. Smoking together seemed to be one of the bonds uniting the crowd at Woodstock.

The use of LSD, a powerful drug which causes hallucinations, is surrounded by a mythology among the hippies. For instance, hippies who favor LSD praise it for its ability to expand consciousness and introduce its users to new sensations. They admit that part of their "trip" consists of images and visions; but more important, they say, is that "acid" also enables them to appreciate new and deeper levels of reality and to experience reality with greater intensity even when they are not "high." LSD users also claim that the drug brings a sense of fusion with all living things and helps its users to relate to people in a more human and sympathetic way.

* See "Drugs and Drug Users" in *Delinquents and Criminals: Their Social World* in this *Readings in Sociology* Series.

However, many users of LSD have had "bad trips." Through too frequent use of the drug, others have become disoriented and have behaved strangely. These are known as "acid freaks." Methedrine, a "pep" pill that speeds up reactions and makes users feel they are bursting with energy, has even more destructive effects on those who employ it regularly. These hippies, whose behavior is often wild and uncontrolled, are known as "speed freaks."

The declining popularity of methedrine among hippies after 1968, together with the hippies' mixed attitudes toward LSD, suggests that hippies use or avoid drugs on the basis of personal experience. Apparently, the hippies who have given up drugs or have kept their use within moderate limits have been deterred not so much by the law as by the effect the drugs have had upon them.

PLASTIC HIPPIES

By rejecting the values of conventional society, particularly those relating to work and business, the hippies found themselves something of an overnight sensation. But ironically, in becoming "hot news," they also became subject to exploitation: they, too, were turned into a product that could be sold in the market place.

As a result of all the publicity and of the opening up of hundreds of "hippie" boutiques, the hippies soon became very popular with novelty-seeking youths. They remain so.* Most of the young consumers show no signs of dropping out of school or work; they are simply attracted to certain features of the hippie adornment and life style which they find daring and exciting: love beads, headbands, Benjamin Franklin (or "Granny") glasses, leather shirts, wild hair styles, a special vocabulary and music—typically ballads sung to the strumming of a guitar. These "hangers-on" are the plastic hippies. On weekends they pour into the hippie haunts such as Greenwich Village in New York, Georgetown in Washington, D.C., and Harvard Square in Cambridge, Massachusetts.

Any movement runs the risk of becoming merely a fad, of being turned into a style without any meaning. The identifying

* See "Fashion: The Rhythm of Change" in this book.

symbols which at first seemed to express genuine outrage at society's injustices and absurdities also became simply stylish objects. By the spring of 1968, the plastic hippie was common in the land, making hippie fashions *the* chosen mode of the most "in" and the most "far-out" youth. And hippie words had penetrated the stage, the newspapers, and TV. Quite conventional adults who like to think they are "with it" readily adopted hippie jargon.

Yet most of the students who dress like hippies still do not share the basic hippie attitudes. Despite appearances, they are still concerned with their future careers and at school they continue to be as grade-conscious as ever. However, in one important respect, the behavior of the plastic hippies overlaps the behavior of the true hippies; many are users of marijuana. Just how much hippie influence has penetrated the youth culture as a whole is not easy to determine.*

MIDNIGHT HIPPIES

Most hippies are in their teens or twenties. Yet there are a significant number of young people who share many of the values of the hippies but who are part of the "straight" world in the sense that they have families and regular jobs. Most of them were in college during the 1950s and were nonconformists by the standards of their time—the not-so-silent minority of the "silent generation."

These midnight, or closet, hippies never dropped out. Quite simply, there was no hippie scene in their time into which they could have dropped. Consequently, they finished school and moved into the job world, usually to fields where there was at least some tolerance of new ideas and unconventional styles of life.

Today, the midnight hippie provides an important link between conformist society and the hippie world. Many conventional people ("squares") find hippies weird, disgusting, or subversive and they can see the justification in any action taken against them. Midnight hippies, on the other hand, because they

---

* See "Middle-Class Delinquency" in *Delinquents and Criminals: Their Social World* in this *Readings in Sociology* Series.

look clean, respectable, and have regular incomes, do not evoke hostility. They can thus voice the hippies' criticisms of life with some hope of gaining a hearing.

THE MEANING OF THE HIPPIE MOVEMENT

The hippie movement has been dismissed as just one more instance of the traditional rebellion of youth against parental authority. Howard, however, concludes from his research that the hippie phenomenon is more important than previous youth movements and that, unlike them, it may have profoundly influenced society as a whole. In distinguishing the hippies from earlier rebellious or bohemian groups, he developed a theory of two types of social deviance: vertical and lateral.

Both kinds of deviance occur in societies where differences of rank exist—such as the differences between officers and recruits, teachers and students, employers and employees, guards and convicts, adults and children. Certain special rights and privileges are accorded the superior ranks. For instance, adults can smoke, drink, drive cars, and vote—things which are forbidden to children and teenagers.

Vertical deviance occurs when persons of the subordinate status attempt to enjoy the privileges and rights of those enjoying superior rank. Thus, when boys drive or drink before they are legally licensed or of age, they are engaging in vertical deviance. And when members of a lower class resort to crime in order to realize middle-class goals, they, too, are engaging in vertical deviance. The point is that this kind of rebel shares the basic values of those he is rebelling against. He simply wants what they already have. In a sense, his rebellion serves to justify the values of the privileged.

In contrast, lateral deviance occurs when persons of the lower rank create their own standards and values. Thus, the teenager who smokes "pot" rather than tobacco is engaging in lateral deviance. So is the 17-year-old girl who runs away to live in a commune, rather than eloping with the boy next door. These rebels do not share their parents' ideas as to what makes the good life. Their values have led them to seek the good life in other things.

In cases of vertical deviance, power remains with the privileged. They are, after all, still recognized by their subordinates as authorities whose lives are worthy of imitation or envy. Therefore, they can control the rule-breaker by gradually extending to him their rights and privileges in exchange for his conformity. They have the power to offer rewards and buy him off.

But in cases of lateral deviance, the privileged do not have this power because, to begin with, the rebel does not want what they have. Therefore, he cannot be talked into abandoning his nonconformist ways. For this reason, parents, adults, or authorities of all types often feel pressed to adopt strong tactics when dealing with lateral deviants, such as the hippie. However, force or persecution only alienate the hippie still further. The result is that he becomes even more committed to his own style of life. And because he cannot be enticed back into normal life, but has found in its place a type of freedom unavailable to the "square," the hippie is a challenge to those still bound to routine from nine to five, five days a week, 52 weeks a year. As a result, the two societies—conformist and nonconformist—become polarized, for there is no agreement on ultimate goals and values.

This, then, is the crucial difference between the hippies and, say, the rebels of the 1920s—the "lost generation"—who were the "swingers" of their era. But basically, the "Babbitts" (as the "squares" of that day were called, after the hero of Sinclair Lewis' best-selling novel of 1924) understood the "bohemians." For the bohemians were just wild youth, trying to live the high life that any normal person might want—if only he could "get away with it." Those rebels did not desire poverty. The values of the two sets were similar. The "lost generation" was an instance of vertical deviance.

The beatniks of the 1950s were not at all like the "lost generation," but, on the contrary, in important features they resembled the hippies of the late sixties and early seventies. In fact, they overlapped the hippies for several years and it is probable that many young people who were beatniks between 1957 and 1960 simply shifted into hippie circles, keeping up with the latest movement among youth. Both are lateral deviants. The two movements share a contempt for the "consumer civilization," a loathing of the role the United States is playing in Southeast Asia, a fierce dedication to the cause of peace, and a tendency to drop out of school or a job which is, to them, irrelevant and even antagonistic to a good life.

But the hippies offer the dropout more than just the warmth of "community." They provide the dropout and the runaway teenager a "pad" in one of their communal households and with it a welcome into a shared way of life.

The hippies' cooperative households have fared better on the land than in the cities. Undoubtedly it is easier to lead their communal life style some distance removed from the critical eyes of the neighbors. But whether on the land or in the city, as long as the communes continue to offer an alternative existence to the disillusioned and the "turned-off," the hippie movement may be in some measure insuring its own survival. It may last longer and wield a more powerful influence on American society than have any of the various youthful protests and revolts that have preceded it.

Black Nationalism*

Under what conditions may a group of oppressed people begin to insist vigorously on their rights?

What is black nationalism? What are its values and goals?

Has black nationalism changed in the United States over the years?

Are today's leaders of the movement like the earlier leaders?
Are there new kinds of people among the followers?

How has the emergence of new nations in Africa affected black nationalism?

An integrated cup of coffee isn't sufficient pay for 400 years of slave labor, and a better job in the white man's factory or position in his business is, at best, only a temporary solution. The only lasting or permanent solution is complete separation on some land that we can call our own.

Malcolm X, December 1, 1963

Policies change, and programs change, according to time. But the objective never changes. . . . Our objective is complete freedom, complete justice, complete equality, by any means necessary.

Malcolm X, December 20, 1964

The assassin's bullet not only killed Dr. King, it killed a period of history. It killed a hope, and it killed a dream.

Eldridge Cleaver, April 6, 1968

Black people are a stolen people held in a colonial status on stolen land, and any analysis which does not acknowledge the colonial status of black people cannot hope to deal with the real problem.

Eldridge Cleaver, April–May, 1968

---

* Adapted from "Black Nationalism" by J. Herman Blake, *The Annals* (Philadelphia: The American Academy of Political and Social Science), Vol. 382 (March 1969), pp. 15–25. Reprinted by permission.

A nationalist consciousness has at last awakened among the black masses of Afro-America. One would have to search far and wide in the annals of history to find a case where such a tide of nationalism did not continue to sweep the people forward into nationhood. . . .

Eldridge Cleaver, April–May, 1968

We do not want a Nation; we are a Nation. We must strengthen and formalize, and play the world's game with what we have, from where we are, as a *truly* separate people.

LeRoi Jones, **Home,** p. 239

These quotations from some of the leading black nationalists of our time give a good idea of the winds blowing through the black community today. Dashikis, Afros, red, green, and black buttons, two-handed greetings, black berets, "soul food" and "soul music" are the more obvious manifestations of this cultural explosion. The signs and sentiments of nationalism are at least familiar to most blacks, whether they are sympathizers or not. But to most whites, such developments are not only frightening—they are beyond understanding. Where, they ask, did this black tornado come from and how could it have struck so suddenly?

J. Herman Blake, a sociologist at the University of California at Santa Cruz, who specializes in the study of black nationalism, would see in this very question an indictment of the way American history has been taught in our schools. For the answer is that black nationalism is not new at all; it has been an almost constant theme in Afro-American history for at least 150 years. How it began, whom it attracted, what forms it has assumed, and where it is heading are among the problems he deals with here.

Slavery was the great contradiction in American society that produced black nationalism. Democracy was introduced into the colonies, but at the same time inequality was also built into the social structure, that is, inequality was institutionalized. From this came the uniqueness of the Afro-American's experience. He was in America, yet not really "American." He alone of all the immigrants to the New World had come unwillingly, in chains. And he, more than any other, was treated as an inferior. Black nationalism is one form of protest against this treatment, as well as a continuing reminder of the ugly contrast between dream and reality in American life.

The first distinctive expression of black nationalism was the desire to separate from America which was voiced by certain free blacks in the early part of the nineteenth century. Convinced that Afro-Americans would never receive justice, these people believed that blacks should leave the country and establish an all-black nation in Africa or in some unclaimed territory. This movement reached its peak in 1854 at a time when slavery appeared permanent. With the Civil War and the Emancipation Proclamation, however, black agitation for emigration ceased, and, with it, the era of *political* nationalism.

Up until the end of Reconstruction, blacks still hoped that they would be permitted to participate fully in American life. But depressing conditions in the South following the withdrawal of Federal troops, together with the limited opportunities available in the North as the result of massive European immigration, soon led the blacks to abandon old hopes. Instead, they developed a new philosophy of self-help.

This new vision called for racial solidarity and economic cooperation to solve Afro-American problems. Booker T. Washington, a leading advocate of *economic* nationalism, felt that if blacks in the rural South received an industrial education and mastered agricultural skills, whites would then realize that black people were worthy of equal treatment. In pursuit of this policy he established the National Negro Business League in 1900 to encourage black enterprises. Unlike political nationalism, economic nationalism was not based on any desire to separate from white society; it was simply a response to white America's rejection of the black.

Cultural nationalism was still another response to the denial of equality to Afro-Americans. It, too, preached racial solidarity. However, this time the stress was on racial pride and dignity fostered by the study of black history and the black's contributions to mankind. Cultural nationalists believed this scholarly approach would give blacks a positive self-image and also show whites that blacks were as good as any other race.

Throughout the nineteenth and early twentieth century,

black nationalist leaders of every stripe came from the upper reaches of the Afro-American community. Martin R. Delany, Booker T. Washington, Arthur A. Schomburg, Carter G. Woodson, and W. E. B. Du Bois were all well-educated men. But the average rural black—the great mass of black Americans—remained untouched by these developments.

TWENTIETH–CENTURY PATTERNS

Conditions were not ripe for a mass movement until after blacks began migrating in large numbers to the industrial cities of the North in the wake of World War I. Here, crowded into slums, they faced a continual round of unemployment, poverty, and bitter hostility from their white neighbors. In short, blacks were just as miserable as ever—with this difference: In the cities, they became more aware of themselves as a community. They realized, too, what a terrible gap lay between their hopes for first-class citizenship and the harsh realities of daily life. Then came Marcus Garvey, a native of Jamaica, bearing a new kind of nationalism and a new kind of hope. With the founding of the Universal Negro Improvement Association (UNIA) in New York in 1917, *integral* nationalism was born.

The UNIA program brought together the various strands of black nationalism. Drawing upon Booker T. Washington's philosophy of economic independence, Garvey established several commercial enterprises, including the Black Star Line, a steamship company designed to link the black people of the world through trade, and the Negro Factories Corporation, designed to build and operate plants in the industrial centers of the United States, Central America, the West Indies, and Africa.

In the tradition of the political nationalists, Garvey sought to have all whites expelled from Africa so that it could become a territory for black people only. He told Afro-Americans that race prejudice was so deeply rooted in white civilization that it was useless to appeal to the white man's sense of justice. Consequently, the only solution was to leave America and return to Africa.

Finally, in the tradition of the cultural nationalists, he vigorously promoted racial solidarity and black consciousness. He urged blacks to look to African history and to be proud of their ancestry. Thus, by fully embracing blackness and fiercely rejecting white America, Garvey avoided the more timid, turn-of-the-century nationalism. He proved a huge success with the urban masses, enjoying a following of at least a half a million in the early 1920s. Though the movement declined after his imprisonment in 1925, integral nationalism by no means died out.

Black nationalism found its next major champion in Elijah Muhammad, who established the Lost Found Nation of Islam in the Wilderness of North America in Detroit in the early 1930s. This movement was small for two decades, but then began to grow rapidly during the 1950s, particularly under the leadership of Malcolm X, a brilliant, reformed and self-taught ex-convict, who was an able organizer and a powerful speaker.

Like the UNIA, the Nation of Islam represents an uncompromising rejection of white America and a turn inward to the black man and the black community as the only source of hope. However, unlike previous black nationalist movements, the Nation of Islam is also a religious sect—with its own holy book (the Koran), set of rituals, beliefs about the end of the world, and hierarchy of authority. The adherents, known as Black Muslims, are strongly evangelistic and puritanical in character.

The cultural nationalism of the Muslims is shown in their rejection of Christianity as the religion of the white man, of the English language, and of the American flag. It also shows up in their refusal to use the term "Negro," to retain family names, or to eat traditional southern foods, all of which they consider reminders of slavery. Black Muslims place great emphasis on black consciousness and racial pride and conduct their search for black identity through the study of Afro-American and African history as well as through the teachings of Islam.

With their emphasis on independent black businesses, Muslims also follow a strong program of economic nationalism. They have set up successful enterprises across the country, including supermarkets supplied with produce from Muslim-owned farms.

Muslims practice political nationalism by insisting on the need of a separate territory for black people. Though they do not specify whether this land should be on the American continent, they argue that since blacks and whites cannot live together in peace, it would be better for blacks to set up an independent nation.

Most ardent black nationalists today have had at least some contact with the Nation of Islam. Yet by the end of the 1960s, the Muslims were no longer in the forefront of the black nationalist struggle. They reached their peak in the early sixties, but declined thereafter with the advances of the Civil Rights Movement —in which Muslims took no part. Many who might otherwise have been attracted to the Muslim program were put off by its doctrine of total separation from America and by its religious emphasis. This was particularly true of college-educated blacks. In sum, the Nation of Islam found its greatest support among the black masses of the urban North.

CONTEMPORARY DEVELOPMENTS

In the one short year of his life between his break with Elijah Muhammad early in 1964 and his assassination in February, 1965, Malcolm X had already gone far to determine the direction black nationalist activity would take during the rest of the decade and into the seventies. Yet the upsurge in nationalist thinking is quite clearly related to several new developments, too.

First of all, the postwar independence movements in Africa and Asia have had a dramatic effect on the thinking of black people. The current generation has seen the rise to sovereignty of dozens of African states. It has witnessed, too, the defeat or humiliation of once-invincible colonial powers in many parts of the world. And it has taken note of the shift in the balance of world power brought about by these changes. All this has increased black pride.

Yet while Africans have gained their independence and have assumed important roles in the United Nations, blacks in the United States still find themselves blocked by the same old barriers. Increasing bitterness over the limited freedom and opportunities of Afro-Americans at home is the result. The gap between black and white citizens remains striking. For example, since 1960, in income and occupational status, black men have not gained much on white males; unemployment has increased; the separation between black communities and white communities has widened; police harassment has continued; and the education of black youth has remained woefully inadequate. Thus, despite certain gains in civil rights, the bread-and-butter issues remain unsolved.

Second, demographic trends in the country have changed the black's position in the nation. The immigration of blacks to the cities first set in motion by World War I has continued unchecked for more than 50 years.* Thus, by 1969, 73 percent of all black people in the United States were residents of the cities, as opposed to 70 percent of the white population who were urbanites. Furthermore, because whites have been moving to the suburbs, more and more of the central cities are becoming all black. For instance, between 1960 and 1965, the proportion of blacks in the inner cities increased by 23 percent, while the proportion of whites in the inner cities declined by nine percent.

But not only is the racial composition of the cities changing; so is the makeup of the blacks who live there. Many of the migrants to central cities are younger blacks who are better educated than the whites who remain in the cities. Furthermore, a new generation is coming to maturity—of young blacks who were born and raised in urban black neighborhoods. The mental framework of these young people is not southern and rural, but is of the American mainstream. Therefore, they are less inclined than their elders to be content with slow progress. Impatience marks their attitude toward their social and economic status.

In addition, the life style of the growing numbers of black youth who complete high school and college is changing. Rather than flee from the inner city, as did successful individuals in the past, these young people are involving themselves in the black community as residents, consumers, and as parents of school children. In this way, a union between intellectuals and the masses has evolved.

All these developments—the heightened interaction of black youth as the result of crowded urban living, the coming of age of a militant, post-World War II generation, and the alliance be-

* See "The Negro Leaves the South" in *Population Growth and the Complex Society;* also "The Negro Family Moves to the City" in *Cities and City Life,* both in this *Readings in Sociology* Series.

tween the intelligentsia and the people—have contributed to the current upsurge in nationalism.

The key figure in the black nationalism of today is still the late Malcolm X. After his break with the Nation of Islam, he began to link the struggle of Afro-Americans with the struggle of oppressed peoples throughout the world, particularly those in Africa. By emphasizing human rights rather than simply civil rights, he raised the hope that the black's situation in America might be made an issue in the United Nations. In short, he made Afro-Americans more aware of the value of connections with the non-Western world.

Toward the end of his life, Malcolm gave new emphasis to the possibility of reform in America. In his speech, "The Ballot or the Bullet," he preached the possibility of a bloodless revolution in this country. This was a departure not only from the despairing views of complete separatists such as Marcus Garvey and Elijah Muhammad but also from earlier views of Malcolm X himself.

Perhaps Malcolm X's great asset was that he was both a man of the people and a penetrating political analyst. Thus he was able to bridge the gap between the masses and the educated minority of blacks. As a first step in attacking racial barriers, he advocated bringing together all black groups in the Organization of Afro-American Unity. For, as he saw it, only as an already strong and united "nation" could the black community negotiate with white America with any hope of success.

Black nationalist activity has quickened since the mid-sixties. Increasing militancy has been the dominant note in almost all groups. A few trends stand out particularly.

The concept of Black Power, first voiced by Stokely Carmichael, is another form of integral nationalism, but with special emphasis on the need for political action and reform measures. Black Power advocates concentrate on community organizing. That is, they have not sought to build a unified mass movement across the country, but rather to develop local programs and policies that reflect the particular needs and conditions of specific communities. They have been active both in the South in voter registration drives and in the northern cities in economic campaigns.

118

The most dramatic development in black nationalist thought, however, is the concern which Malcolm X expressed with the issues of colonization of black people. These include problems of land, self-determination for black communities, and the accountability of black leaders. Influenced by both Malcolm X and the writings of Frantz Fanon, a black interpreter of the struggles of native colonial Algerians to free themselves from France, black intellectuals are teaching the connection between the oppression of colonial peoples and the oppression of blacks in America.

Controlled by forces from outside the black communities (for example, the police and welfare departments), the plight of the large numbers of blacks in central cities bears a strong resemblance to a colonial situation. Many blacks realize that such urban concentrations are similar to colonized nations. They argue that residents of black communities should view the territory they occupy as their own. More and more they are demanding local self-determination for black communities.

In turn, the emphasis on self-determination has led to the principle of accountability. That is, those who hold positions of power which affect the black community should answer exclusively to the black community. This is a rule of the Black Panther Party, whose leaders constitute a sort of government-in-exile and whose members assume responsibility for their constituencies by running free food and medical programs and by organizing the defense of black residents against police harassment. In 1968 the Panthers also entered national politics by forming a coalition with the Peace and Freedom Party.

The main thrust of cultural nationalism is the campaign by black students to set up black studies programs on college campuses throughout the country. These courses of study, however, are designed as supports of the black community rather than as wholly academic pursuits. Together with the emphasis on black as beautiful, they have brought black consciousness to a level never before achieved.

WHERE WILL ALL THESE TRENDS LEAD?

Economic nationalism survives and thrives here and there where black businessmen flourish. There are some notably successful black enterprises. However, the lack of capital and of commercial and industrial experience are formidable handicaps which black merchants and manufacturers may take years to surmount. That blacks have done better in certain of the professions is due to the fact that the white practitioners had no very strong desire to compete for black patronage. But improvements in other aspects of the life of blacks—for example, in education—may have the effect of encouraging their economic development.

Cultural nationalism may grow apace in the last decades of this century which has brought much change to black America. The media of communication serve the black community more adequately than ever before. This raises the interesting question: Will the better flow of news and information divide the races or integrate them?

Blake maintains that political nationalism is expanding. And he asks the fundamental question: Will the barrier of skin color defy every effort to make America one united nation? If so, political nationalism can be expected to grow stronger and more radical.

The Student Protesters*

Against what social values do students protest?

What changes in these values would student activists like to see?

Are all students involved in student protest: in demonstrations, sit-ins, and picketing?

What is the difference in family background between the protesters and the others?

From what is the "liberated" generation liberated?

Are the values of the "liberated" generation likely to become generally accepted?

TV Newsman: What did you students hope to gain by this takeover of the Dean's office here at State University?

Jeff Greenblatt, Student leader: We wanted to call attention to the policies of the university which are directly helping the war. We want the university to cancel its defense contracts and to stop all research connected with the war.

Jeff Greenblatt may be typical of the white, college-age protesters of the sixties and seventies. The son of a corporation lawyer, he grew up in Livingston, New Jersey. He graduated from high school in the top ten of his class and easily won admittance to the state university. In his first two years, Jeff ranked near the top of his class and was active in clubs and athletics. In his Junior year, however, Jeff became more and more involved in political action groups and contributed regularly to the campus underground publication, *The Rotten Onion*. In the spring of his Junior

* Adapted from "The Liberated Generation: An Exploration of the Roots of Student Protest" by Richard Flacks, *Journal of Social Issues*, Vol. XXIII, No. 3 (1967), pp. 56–57, 65–68, 71–72. Reprinted by permission.

year, he led a group of fellow radicals in the three-day occupation of the Dean's office to protest the university's undertaking of defense-related research. Jeff's role in the sit-in resulted in his suspension from the university. During his year off, Jeff lived near the campus and continued to write for the *Onion*. He also worked at organizing an even more radical group of students called "the Garbagemen."

> *Newsman:* But how can the university afford to cut off the funds brought in by defense contracts?
> *Jeff G.:* The university will have to afford it! If this school is going to preach peace and humanitarism in its classrooms, then it must practice the same policies in its labs!

To Jeff Greenblatt and other student activists—that is, the students who actually participate in the strikes, marches, and takeovers—protest has become a way of life with its own set of values. The values have determined the themes of protest for a decade and a half. They have been named and analyzed by Richard Flacks, who was a professor of sociology at the University of Chicago at the time of a student demonstration there. These values include

1. Romanticism. Most of the activists have a strong desire to lead a "free life"—one not bound by conventional feelings, expressions, or experiences. Many of them yearn for the old romantic ideal—to "know and experience all things."

2. Anti-Authoritarianism. The activists are strongly opposed to arbitrary rules or regulations and to the making of decisions or manipulating by any "higher authority."

3. Populism or Egalitarianism. The activists also strongly believe in the right of all men to participate in government. They believe the real power of society rests with the common people—the masses—not with the elite or with the "party politicians."

4. Anti-Dogmatism. The activists strongly object to any formulas, models, or plans for arranging the social structure. They are opposed to the "Establishment," because it maintains things in the way they are. The famous phrase "Don't trust anyone over thirty" really means "Don't trust the old ideas and ways; look for new ways."

5. Moral Purity. The activists also are greatly opposed to any actions which benefit one individual at the expense of other individuals. They reject traditional forms of business and they accuse the capitalistic system of exploiting the weak and uneducated. At the university level, the activists argue that activities such as research connected with war and national defense destroy the school's morals.

6. *Community and Communication.* Throughout the movement, the activists place great emphasis on "human relationships." Most feel they must fully express their emotions and feelings to communicate, even if they violate the traditional standards of sexual morality, racial mixing, and so on. They demand, for example, that the campus "community" be changed to allow for more direct contact or "communication" between student and teacher.

7. *Anti-Institutionalism.* Finally, most activists express a great distrust of society's conventional institutions—the business corporation, the military, the church, the mass media, and even the university. Almost all activists say they wish to avoid "institutional" careers in industry, science, or politics. Instead, they hope to continue to work in the movement or to become freelance writers or artists.

> *Newsman:* Do many of the other students share your ideas and ideals, Jeff?
>
> *Jeff G.:* Of course, not all of them do. But most of my friends think the way I do. Most of them believe we are doing the right thing.

At the University of Chicago during 1965 and 1966, Professor Flacks undertook a series of studies of parents and of students, some of whom were active in protest demonstrations and others of whom were not active. He learned, for one thing, that the activists, on the whole, shared each other's values and ideals. They also came from fairly similar backgrounds. The most radical and most deeply involved of the activists usually were exceptionally bright, talented students.

The activist students whom he interviewed more often reported high family incomes and high levels of family education than did the control group of nonactivist students. The activists also more often perceived of themselves as "upper middle class."

In one sample of students, half of the 24 who came from families with incomes of over $15,000 participated in sit-ins or similar protests. On the other hand, only two students out of the 23 reporting family incomes of under $15,000 had ever joined in a campus demonstration.

Flacks also found that the parents of activists are more likely to be professionals (lawyers, college faculty, doctors) than salesmen, businessmen, white-collar or blue-collar workers. More of their mothers, too, are employed, usually in well-paying professional careers.

Many among the activists reported that their grandparents were foreign born. The grandparents, on the whole, were more highly educated than the grandparents of nonactivists. In other words, the tradition of education and high social standing of the activists' families often stretched back several generations.

> *Newsman:* Does your father approve of this protest, Jeff? Or has he taken any steps to stop you?
> *Jeff G.:* I think my father agrees with my point of view. At least he hasn't tried to stop me.

Looking beyond merely the outward accomplishments of the activists' families, Flacks found that the social and political tone of their homes was not at all like that in the homes of the nonactivists. For one thing, the activists' fathers were not quite as radical as their offspring, but they were much more liberal than the fathers of nonactivists.

In a sampling of parental politics, Flacks found that 40 percent of the nonactivists' fathers were registered Republicans. Moreover, 40 percent of these fathers thought of themselves as "conservatives." By contrast, only 13 percent of the activists' fathers were registered Republicans, and not one considered himself a "conservative."

Generally, the attitudes of fathers and sons in various political issues of the late 1960s ran parallel to each other (Table 1). In fact that pattern was the same in both camps.

Most activists came from very liberal homes and were likely to be more liberal than their fathers. Many of the nonactivist students were conservative, like their fathers, but even *more* so. Perhaps the student protesters are not really rebelling against

TABLE 1

TABLE 1
Students' and Fathers' Attitudes on Issues

ISSUE	ACTIVISTS:		NONACTIVISTS:	
	STUDENTS	FATHERS	STUDENTS	FATHERS
Percent Who Approve:				
Bombing of North Vietnam	9%	27%	73%	80%
American Troops in Dominican Republic	6	33	65	50
Student Participation in Protest Demonstrations	100	80	61	37
Civil Disobedience in Civil Rights Protests	97	57	28	23
Congressional Investiga- of "Un-American Activities"	3	7	73	57
Lyndon Johnson	35	77	81	83
Barry Goldwater	0	7	35	20
Full Socialization of Industry	62	23	5	10
Socialization of the Medical Profession	94	43	30	27

parental opinions.* Indeed Flacks points out that they seem to be supporting and fulfilling the political traditions of their families.

> *Newsman:* Your father is a successful lawyer, Jeff. Doesn't he want you to follow in his footsteps?
> *Jeff G.:* I think my father wants me to do what is right.

In addition to the political similarity between fathers and sons, Flacks also found that student activism is related to a com-

---

* See "Politics and the Rebellious Adolescent" in *Life in Families* in this *Readings in Sociology* Series.

plex system of values and philosophies fostered in a student's family.

The nonactivists and their parents tended to express rather conventional views of success, achievement, sexual morality, and religion. By contrast, both the activists and their parents placed higher values on intellectual and artistic interests, on humanitarian work, and on self-expression. Moreover, both activist students and their parents played down the importance of a career, personal wealth, conventional morality, and religion.

For example, when asked to rank the most important "areas of life," the nonactivists most often placed marriage, career, and religion near the top of the list. The activists, on the other hand, ranked these goals much lower than "the world of ideas, art, and music" or "work for national and international betterment."

Finally, Flacks tried to find how different the two kinds of parents had been in rearing their children. First he asked the students certain questions bearing on the seven values he had discovered among the activists. On the basis of their replies, he labeled some, for convenience, "Hi-activist" and the others "Lo-activist." Hi-activists, of course, were those who appeared most deeply committed to the activist values. And Lo-activists were those who were least enthusiastic about the values.

Then Flacks asked the students to rate "how my mother (father) treated me as a child" on various scales of values: mild-stern, soft-hard, lenient-severe, easy-strict. He sorted out the replies of the Hi-activists from those of the Lo-activists and thus was able to compare the two groups (Table 2). This procedure revealed the fact that the activists in general consistently rate their parents as "milder," "more lenient," and less "severe."

When all of Flacks' data are put together to make a composite picture, the typical white student activist of the middle 1960s turns out to be very much like the fictional Jeff Greenblatt of State University. He comes from a family that is urban, highly educated, and probably not affiliated with any religious denomination. His family is also liberal, intellectual, permissive, and comfortable as to income. In short, the student who most often participates in attacks on the Establishment is also the very student who could most easily achieve all the social and career goals which the Establishment honors.

TABLE 2
Ratings of Parents by Children

CHILD'S RATING OF PARENT:	SONS		DAUGHTERS	
	Hɪ-Act	Lo-Act	Hɪ-Act	Lo-Act
Mild-Stern				
Percent Rating Mother "Mild"	63%	44%	59%	47%
Percent Rating Father "Mild"	48	33	48	32
Soft-Hard				
Percent Rating Mother "Soft"	69	61	60	57
Percent Rating Father "Soft"	50	50	62	51
Lenient-Severe				
Percent Rating Mother "Lenient"	94	61	66	63
Percent Rating Father "Lenient"	60	44	47	42
Easy-Strict				
Percent Rating Mother "Easy"	75	50	77	52
Percent Rating Father "Easy"	69	44	47	37

Newsman: Why should the son of a well-to-do, upper-middle-class family revolt against all that American society seems to stand for?

Jeff G.: I don't know. Maybe it's because we think that the standards of that society are wrong.

Flacks offers one suggestion to explain why so many middle-class youths have chosen to protest against the conventional standards of society. He concludes that a new type of life style has been developing among a broad segment of the upper middle class in the last third of the twentieth century. Today, in many of these families, there is great emphasis on democratic personal relationships between parents and children. In short, children are no longer simply "seen and not heard." They take part in family discussions, help make family decisions, and often contribute to the intellectual climate of family life.

In these families, too, there is a high standard of what is morally right, according to which the children are expected to govern their own behavior. This means that children can express themselves emotionally and creatively. Thus they may be allowed to violate conventions concerning dating, dress, and mode of speech. Yet they are to a large extent free to decide for themselves what is morally right and wrong; their parents expect them to be concerned about social issues.

Moreover, these families have established new values of achievement and success. They reject material goals, such as a large income, a big car, or a house in the country. Rather, children are taught that intellectual achievement, artistic creation, political involvement, or simply self-discovery are the important goals in life.

At the same time, however, these children are comfortable, have no worries, are well educated, and are given all the material things they want. Thus, as they grow older, the traditional rewards of wealth or social status are not things still to be won.

In short, the past decade has produced a truly liberated generation of youth with both the impulse to free themselves from convention and tradition—and the money and the backing which allow them to do so.

In contrast, conventional parents are more likely to stress personal self-control and to be somewhat indifferent to social and political questions. Ironically, while the American family has become smaller, closer, more personal, more democratic, and more liberal, American society has become larger, more complex, more bureaucratic, more confusing, and more impersonal than ever. Young people raised in upper-middle-class, comfortable, liberal homes find it more and more difficult to accept the arbitrary and, to them, often senseless rules of established institutions. Brought up in a free, liberal atmosphere, the younger generation cannot understand why so many members of the older generation continue to cling to the conventional values of status, competition, sexual morality, religion, race prejudice, dress, and to a host of other taboos and traditions.

Newsman: Surely, you don't believe that the school administration is going to bow to the demands of a group of students?

Jeff G.: Why not? The school is supposed to exist for the students, isn't it? We are the most important part of the educational process, aren't we?

Newsman: Then this protest actually goes beyond just the issue of defense contracts?

Jeff G.: I suppose it does. We want a voice in the university's affairs as they affect our lives.

Newsman: If this protest is successful, will you stage others in the future?

Jeff G.: We'll keep on protesting until justice is done and all our demands are met.

The Radical Right*

How is the social and economic position of individuals who join the Ku Klux Klan similar to the position of those who join the John Birch Society or the Minutemen?

What social conditions have favored the growth of the radical right since World War II?

What values do organizations of the radical right have in common?

What is the difference between the values held by organizations of the radical left, such as the Communist party, and organizations of the radical right?

Tommy Lee Baker, 35, of Tuscaloosa, Alabama; white, machinist, married and the father of three children, veteran, and a member of the White Knights of the Ku Klux Klan.

Rocco Mancini, 42, of Newark, New Jersey; white, factory worker, married and the father of four children, and a member of the North Ward Citizens Committee.

Rodney Hamilton, 24, of Los Angeles, Califronia; white, plasterer, single, veteran, and a member of the Minutemen.

Three men—a racist of the South, an urban vigilante of the North, and an anti-Communist guerrilla of the West—thousands of miles apart, yet side by side in their social and political views.

All three men share the vague sense of alienation felt by many members of the American working class. All three express dark feelings of prejudice. All three men act out the violent tendencies in the American character. And all three are the products of fear and confusion in a changing world.

All three men are white, militant radicals of the right.

---

* Adapted from "White Militancy" by Jerome H. Skolnick, *The Politics of Protest* (New York: Simon and Schuster, 1969), pp. 218–236. Reprinted by permission.

THE WHITE RACISTS

"You have to be black to get a welfare check
And I'm broke/No joke
I ain't got a nickel for a coke
I ain't black you see. . . ."
—Selection from a Klan songbook

Tommy Lee Baker dropped out of school in the eleventh grade to enlist in the Air Force. Trained as a mechanic in the service, Tommy Lee thought he would get a civilian job with an airline ground crew. Unfortunately, such jobs are hard to find in Alabama, and Tommy Lee worked as a bricklayer, a truck driver, and a construction helper before he finally found a steady job as a machinist.

During one of his long periods of unemployment, Tommy Lee started going to Klan meetings, just to kill time. But then he soon grew serious about the Klan. He liked what the members of the Klan were trying to do. And he liked the other fellows in the Klan; they were very much like him. For example, the top leadership in recent years had included a truck driver, a crane operator, a barber, a former lightning rod salesman, a paint sprayer, a bricklayer, a rubber plant worker, and several evangelical ministers.

The things that they said made sense to Tommy Lee. He had had a hard time finding a job and the Klan told him why. They said it was because all that job assistance and antipoverty money was going to the lawbreaking blacks, while law-abiding, poor whites were getting no federal help at all.

The Ku Klux Klan has grown out of the special conditions in the South. In recent years, major social and economic changes have produced a dispossessed and insecure group of marginal whites on the bitter edge between poverty and prosperity. Although industrialization has helped create a more affluent and liberal middle class during the past several decades, it has brought no help to many poor, uneducated whites.*

---

* See "Who Is Against Desegregation?" in *Racial and Ethnic Relations* in this *Readings in Sociology* Series.

The same industrialization, for one thing, has helped break down the old caste system that kept the blacks in bondage.* Moreover, many blacks have moved into the cities and taken new jobs in factories, as well as many formerly "white" jobs in stores and offices. At the same time, the civil rights laws have increased the blacks' political power and reduced the old controls once held by whites. All of these changes add to the insecurity, fear, and sense of powerlessness shared by the poor whites of the South. In this atmosphere of change and confusion, the Ku Klux Klan represents the last stand of traditional white supremacy. It is no surprise, then, that the Klan members are mainly marginal, small businessmen and semi-skilled workers. They are men on the borderline between clear-cut white-collar and blue-collar jobs, with little security beyond their next paychecks and no future.

The Klan seems to be secretly backed (or at least, silently supported) by middle-class racists who have a serious stake in maintaining the old economic system and the caste traditions.

With other militant white groups, the Klan is set up apparently to do the "dirty work" of the Establishment. Ironically, the white terrorists help support a political and economic climate in which the poor of *both races* suffer. Indeed, it is said that the Establishment fears war between the races less than it fears an alliance between them.

THE URBAN VIGILANTES

"We have learned from the black people that the squeaky wheel gets the grease, so we're going to squeak, too."

—Tony Imperiale, Newark, New Jersey

During the 1960s, white militancy began rising in the big cities of the West and North, first against blacks, and later against youthful antiwar demonstrators.

Militancy developed as a white backlash to the black movement to secure civil rights, the ghetto riots, and rising crime rates. Actually, the real causes are related to the causes of southern racism: the insecurity and fear of the working-class whites.

* See "Caste in India and in the United States" in *Racial and Ethnic Relations* in this *Readings in Sociology* Series.

CROWD AND MASS BEHAVIOR

Rocco Mancini is a member of the North Ward Citizens Committee, a neighborhood vigilante group in Newark, New Jersey. Rocco grew up in Newark, the son of immigrant parents. He has lived there all his life in the Italian North Ward. His Newark has changed much in 40 years. The city has decayed. The North Ward has become surrounded by black ghettos.

Rocco works hard to support his wife and four children on his salary of $8000. He has no capital, no stocks, and no real estate except his house in the North Ward. Actually, he would like to move, but he still owes money on the mortgage, the car, and the household appliances.

Rocco is an active union member, but this does not mean his job is secure. His factory has frequent layoffs, and a rumor has been in the air lately that the plant may move out of Newark. Moreover, his taxes are high, neighborhood services are poor, his health is wretched, and he has no political power in the city. Thus, Rocco feels his situation is desperate. He is just above the subsistence level of poverty. He is afraid of the nearby black ghetto. He is afraid to walk in the streets at night. And he does not want to send his children by bus to what may be inferior schools in another part of town.

In short, Rocco sees only one possible outcome of the civil rights movement—the loss of his home, his job, and his children's future. He is anxious and frightened. And he reacts with violent talk and sometimes with violent action.

Luckily, the white militancy in the urban North so far has been mainly talk. Polls show that over 50 percent of the gun-owning whites say they would shoot to kill during a riot. But only a few isolated instances of whites attacking blacks have actually been reported. Most of the actual white violence against blacks has been from youths. Outbreaks of violence in racially mixed schools have become commonplace in many big American cities.

But the potential for adult violence exists in the so-called neighborhood defense leagues. The "Breakthrough" organization in Detroit urges members to arm themselves, study warfare, and stock their pantries with provisions. Another group called "Fight Back" in Warren, Michigan, claims: "The only way to stop them is at the city limits."

Perhaps the best known of these groups is the North Ward Citizens Committee of Newark, led by a member of the city council whose Italian forefathers a generation ago were at the bottom of the social and economic ladder and were discriminated against by native Americans. Today, the situation is reversed. The North Ward Italians themselves feel endangered by "criminal blacks led by student radicals." The vigilantes of the North Ward Citizens Committee organize patrols of the neighborhood, carry weapons, and train themselves in karate, a Japanese mode of self-defense.

Oddly enough, the complaints of the white ethnic groups in the North sound very much like the complaints of the Klan in the South. According to one North Warder: "The Negro gets all the anti-poverty money. Are there no poor whites? When pools are built in the Central Ward (the black section), don't they think white kids have got frustrations, too? You know how many white kids can't get a job? They have been told, 'we have to hire Negroes first!'"

As debate over the Vietnam War increased in the late 1960s, and as the much-discussed gap * between generations deepened, the vague fears of the working-class whites—children of foreign-born parents or grandparents—expanded to include liberals, students, antiwar critics, and almost all long-haired youths.

THE PARAMILITARY RIGHTISTS

See the old man at the corner where you buy your papers? He may have a silencer equipped pistol under his coat. That extra fountain pen in the pocket of the insurance salesman who calls on you might be a cyanide gas gun. What about your milkman? Arsenic works slow but sure. Your auto mechanic may stay up nights studying booby traps. These patriots are not going to let you take their freedom away. . . . Traitors, beware! Even now the cross hairs are on the back of your necks.

—a Minutemen Message

Right-wing reaction against the left is nothing new in America.

* See "Whose Generation Gap?" in this book.

During the great "Red Scare" following World War I, the United States Attorney General led a massive campaign of arrest and harassment of foreigners, liberals, and union leaders suspected of "Communist" leanings. President Franklin Roosevelt and his wife were condemned for their "Communist sympathies." And, in the 1950s, Senator Joe McCarthy conducted his famous "witch hunts" for suspected Reds in government.

Although McCarthy was denounced and discredited, the fight was continued in secrecy by a number of anti-Communist organizations. The most famous of these is the John Birch Society. The Birch Society under the leadership of Robert Welch attracted influential, well-to-do businessmen and industrialists. For many years, the Birch Society was effective in opposing liberal politicians, particularly at a local level.

While the Birch Society drew its members from the more "respectable" upper-middle-class branch of the ultraconservative, right-wing movement, a number of other far-right groups appealed to the lower levels. These paramilitary groups advocate a full-fledged, armed conflict against the leftists.

The members of the paramilitary groups seem to be for the most part men who can neither explain their grievances against the system, nor apply their energies to any normal political program. Instead, they feel that direct action alone can bring back their vague, undefined, idealized "real America."

Rodney Hamilton grew up in a small Iowa town. After high school he entered the Army and served in Vietnam. He believed deeply in the American cause. When he was wounded, he was proud to have been defending democracy.

Rodney returned to civilian life with a Purple Heart medal, a limp, no particular vocational skills, and a grudging hatred of Communism. He settled in Los Angeles because his uncle ran a plastering company there. One day, an old Army buddy asked Rodney if he would like to join an organization, the Minutemen, devoted to "defending the American way of life." His buddy said they needed men with combat experience. Rodney gladly joined.

The Minutemen grew out of several smaller guerrilla organizations that flowered in the late 1950s. During that period, the whole country seemed to be in the throes of the Cold War and the fear that the Communists would conquer the world.

In one sense, the aims of the Minutemen were not very different from goals then expressed by the Federal government. Indeed, their original purpose—to provide guerrilla training in the event of an armed invasion by the Russians—might even be seen as a logical extension of the policies of national security that gave birth to universal military training and the National Guard.

From this logical beginning, however, the Minutemen gradually became more and more possessed with the illogical idea that Communists had taken over the United States government and the direction of American foreign policy. The Minutemen believe that Communists have infiltrated every Federal agency and are only waiting for "the day of revolution." When that day comes, the Minutemen feel they will be the "last line of defense."

The Minutemen's membership in 1970 probably was no more than 8000 men, scattered in tiny bands throughout the United States, with heavy concentrations on the West Coast. These small and semi-autonomous cells train for guerrilla warfare through drills, seminars, and an occasional real-life attack on the liberal enemy. Minutemen-linked events have included the robbing of a bank, the dynamiting of police and power stations near Seattle, the assaulting of peace groups in New York and Connecticut, and the bombing of liberal radio stations in the Southwest.

One of the reasons why Rodney Hamilton liked this organization was that the other members were much like himself: white, predominantly young, of western-European descent, Christian, and economically lost in the gray area between the blue-collar and the white-collar class. For example, the founder and leader of the Minutemen is a Midwestern businessman who had suffered financial failure. Among other known Minutemen are longshoremen, grocery clerks, ship's oilers, handymen, truck drivers, and owners of small, marginal businesses. Obviously, the socioeconomic character of the Minutemen is very much like that of the Klansmen, and even somewhat similar to that of the ethnic vigilantes of the cities.

Although the Minutemen are not particularly anti-Semitic or antiblack, the small-town whites who are its members suffer social strains similar to those of the Klansmen and the urban vigilantes. For the small-town businessman, the urban clerk, and the marginal worker—to name a few typical members—is often overwhelmed by social developments beyond his ability to control or understand. In a very real sense, he is not threatened by Communism as much as he is threatened by the new shape of modern capitalism. The typical Minuteman wants to return to the frontier style of capitalism identified with "free enterprise" and "individualism," when a man with a few dollars and some ambition could make a good living. Today's brand of big corporation capitalism has left him behind. His little one- or two-man company cannot compete with the giants who "get all the tax breaks," the government contracts, and the controlled markets. In addition, the Federal and the state governments have grown so big that he cannot even understand them, let alone avail himself of their help.

CONCLUSION

Tommy Lee Baker, Rocco Mancini, and Rodney Hamilton—three men from three different parts of the country with three different goals. Yet, all three represent a single point of view. Indeed, with a little shift in geography, any one of them might have joined any of the other organizations. All three are working-class whites caught between the "old America" and the "new America." All three respond to the resulting social stresses with the same reaction—violence!

For decades, the white militants have represented the rough edge of a deeper, more widespread, national distrust of Indians and foreigners, immigrants and blacks, liberals and intellectuals. The violence of the extremist groups fits into the history and, to a great extent, the outlook of the American people.* In fact, it may be suspected that these groups give expression to sentiments silently and secretly held by a near majority of white American citizens.

Ku Klux Klan leaders openly admit that their strength comes from favorable public opinion. "As long as the people are on our side," says one, "we can do just about anything to our enemies we want."

* See "Riots: Past and Present Violence" in *Delinquents and Criminals: Their Social World* in this *Readings in Sociology* Series.

A poll of public opinion taken after the campus violence at Kent State in 1970 showed a significant number of Americans thought the "students got what they deserved." Similar public statements of support followed the police riot in Chicago at the Democratic National Convention of 1968 and after the hard-hat construction workers attacked student demonstrators on Wall Street in 1970.

Will the Tommy Lee Bakers, Rocco Mancinis, and Rodney Hamiltons remain scattered, small examples of the darker instincts in the American character? Or will they multiply, rallying white against black, right against left, old against young? The answers to these questions depend on how well the social-political system of the future can satisfy the demands and calm the fears of opposed sections of the population.

When Disaster Strikes*

How do people and groups act in the face of extreme stress?

Is "panic" a real problem in a disaster?

What are the problems of human behavior which emergency planners must deal with in a catastrophe?

Are there differences in human reactions to wartime and peacetime crises?

SOMEWHERE IN FRANCE

It started in mid-May in Flanders and went on for the next six weeks. A significant part of the French population was caught up in the vast migration. This was the great debacle of 1940. The peasants in northern France began the exodus. Remembering the German occupation of 1914–18, they chose not to live through a second round. And so, as the panzers moved closer, in fear and haste they packed up as many of their belongings as they could load on farm wagons and headed south.

As they proceeded, their arrival alerted each new town in its turn, so that soon the inhabitants of hundreds of villages joined in the precipitous flight to "safety." By June 10, when the French government left the threatened capital, much of Paris had rushed to join them. In time, the main roads of France were clogged by a never-ending stream of often balky automobiles, rickety bicycles, horse-drawn vehicles, and assorted pedestrians—a human tide that interfered with the movements of the hard-pressed French army. Moreover, it was a perfect target for the German dive bombers which terrorized a civilian population already close to total collapse. Much as the Nazis hoped, panic succeeded in softening up the French. The French leaders requested the cessation of hostilities just a week after the government left Paris.

---

* Adapted from "Images of Withdrawal Behavior in Disasters: Some Basic Misconceptions" by Enrico L. Quarantelli, *Social Problems* (South Bend, Indiana: The Society for the Study of Social Problems), Vol. 8, No. 1 (Summer 1960), pp. 68–78. Reprinted by permission.

Chicago, 1903

The final tally of the dead came to 602. Yet from start to finish, the catastrophe lasted only eight minutes. By the time the fire chief entered the Iroquois Theater, everyone had either escaped or perished. Just about everything that might have gone wrong that grim December day did go wrong. Someone in the audience had yelled "Fire"—which precipitated the panicky surge to the doors. The asbestos safety curtain—which would have confined the fire to the stage where it had started—failed to work. The central lights went off at a crucial moment. The 30 exits proved hard to find and many of the doors were jammed. In their frenzy, people jumped or fell from the fire escapes to their deaths on the pavement below; inside the theater, those up in the balcony stampeded on the stairways, and their trampled bodies piled up in mounds. When it was over hundreds were found mangled, crushed, or smothered to death. It was a disaster that surpassed in horror almost anything that had ever happened in an American city—a classic of its kind.

These are the types of scenes that are inevitably recalled whenever people think of crowd behavior in the face of disaster. Yet these incidents may have become famous precisely because they were not typical. Both—at least according to the popular accounts of them—involved disorganized masses, panic, irrationality, and antisocial impulses.

Drawing upon his studies of crowd behavior, and adding to them the findings of other sociologists, Enrico Quarantelli, a sociologist at Ohio State University and a former member of the Disaster Team of the National Opinion Research Center, constructed a description of how a typical crowd is likely to behave in the face of disaster. Then he discovered that official relief agencies, including police and fire departments, the Red Cross, and civilian defense organizations, all shared certain misconceptions about behavior under stress. To refute these misconceptions Quarantelli wrote a paper on the sociological theory of the impact of disaster. It reveals both the expected things that do not happen and unexpected things that do happen during a disaster.

To begin with, Quarantelli explains, most relief organizations assume that the victims of a disaster will withdraw as soon as

CROWD AND MASS BEHAVIOR

possible from the place of danger, that is, the "impact area." This assumption, in turn, is based on three more beliefs which are highly questionable: that disaster victims will be seized by "panic"; that they will be in a "dependent" condition; and that they will be capable of being "controlled" by outside agencies bringing aid.

THE IMAGE OF "PANIC"

In any catastrophe the disaster workers are accustomed to make their plans in terms of the widespread personal and social chaos they expect. Indeed, responsible officials are so convinced of the reality of the "panic syndrome" that they frequently fail to take appropriate measures before the disaster has actually struck. They fear bringing about just such panic conditions. Thus, despite the urgent recommendations of the Weather Bureau and Coast Guard, city officials and state police refused to order the people to leave an eastern ocean resort because they feared such action would precipitate a panicky flight from the predicted violent hurricane. In like manner, alarm bells were not rung on the collision-doomed ship, the "Andrea Doria," for fear of spreading panic among the passengers.

It is also commonly assumed that a population will inevitably flee in confusion from a disaster area in the event of enemy air attack. The chief problem, it is supposed, is to stop a panicky exodus and to evacuate a city in such a way that order will be preserved and a rout prevented.

However, nothing of the kind took place during the Battle of Britain in 1940 or during the German rocket attacks on England in 1944. On the contrary, people showed great reluctance to leave the danger zones. For example, only 37 percent of the total number of mothers and children who were able to leave London actually went. Thus the problem was actually one of getting people to move rather than of preventing their flight. Apparently, there is a strong human tendency to continue what one is doing rather than to start a new course of activity, no matter what the circumstances.

Where the disaster threat is slow-moving, as with floods, the tendency to stay put actually poses a major problem for control officials. Reports of floods in America, Mexico, Britain, Holland, and Italy consistently mention the reluctance of the threatened people to withdraw from the endangered area—even in the face of threats or coercive measures. The same unwillingness to leave threatened locations is also true of the victims or potential victims of maritime catastrophes, avalanches, air raids, violent explosions, and long-term epidemics.

In fact, even when their physical world is literally disintegrating around them, substantial numbers of individuals often refuse to withdraw from the danger area. For instance, Bootle, England, a city of 55,000, was bombed nightly for a week during World War II. Only ten percent of all houses escaped serious damage. Nevertheless, a fourth of the inhabitants chose to sleep in their own houses during the raids—despite the fact that community facilities were shattered, all main roads were blocked, gas and water works were a shambles, and the distribution of food was badly disrupted.

People not only do not run from danger; those who leave sometimes return even though the threat persists. For instance, in World War II in Nazi Germany, even children were brought back to danger zones although the government, to discourage their return, refused to provide them with school or ration cards.

Nor are the scenes of pandemonium, chaos, and panic so frequently reported in journalistic and popular accounts borne out by the scientific studies. This discrepancy, Quarantelli believes, lies in the failure of nonscientific observers to distinguish between personal and social disorganization. In other words, when disaster strikes relatively widespread social or community disorganization can be found together with a lack of disorganization at the level of the individual and the small group. Thus, for instance, when the Rio Grande overflowed its banks, less than five percent of the 30,000 evacuees from Piedras Negras, Mexico, were helped by any sort of organization, and at Eagle Pass on the American side only four percent were evacuated by officials. Yet the inhabitants acted deliberately and rationally and gave assistance to their relatives, friends, and neighbors so that an orderly withdrawal from the area was accomplished.

There is also frequent failure to recognize that involved individuals and groups are often acting in response to different conceptions of the disaster situation. Thus, from the vantage point of an airplane, the behavior exhibited by people withdrawing from their homes during a series of house explosions in a Rochester, New York, suburb might well have appeared chaotic and irrational; but from the perspective of the crowd, the withdrawal was relatively controlled, logical, and well adjusted to the specific circumstances. The people had "used their heads," discussed the merits of various plans for withdrawing to areas of safety, and then acted on their decisions.

Still another reason why the image of panic is so prevalent in descriptions of disaster is that reporters often fail to differentiate between simple flight and panic. In a true panicky flight, such as occurred at the Iroquois Theater, the individual loses all sense of responsibility to anyone but himself and concentrates exclusively on escaping what he perceives as imminent death. But such events are rare. In most kinds of flights, individuals continue to play their usual social roles and remain mindful of their obligations to family and friends. Flight in itself cannot be taken as a sign of panic because in many instances it is quite obviously the only sensible response to impending danger.

THE IMAGE OF "DEPENDENCY"

Another conception common among professional relief personnel is that of the passivity or "dependency" of disaster victims. After being officially guided to safety, the victims will, it is thought, be so shocked, discouraged, apathetic, and lacking in initiative that everything will have to be done for them. Quarantelli admits that this "disaster syndrome" does sometimes appear following sudden and very violent catastrophes. But he argues that it affects only a limited number of those victimized and that it usually does not last long.

Contrary to popular belief, disaster victims are likely to respond actively to their circumstances. They do not just wait for offers of help from organizations. They act on their own. Sometimes they even act in a way contrary to the expressed wishes of formal agencies and public authorities. And they quickly begin to establish patterns of informal mutual aid.

In general, disaster victims work out their own private arrangements for withdrawing from the area of impact and for finding shelter. For example, when a tornado hit Worcester, Massachusetts, approximately 10,000 persons were made homeless. However, only about 50 individuals were housed by the public authorities. The vast majority of displaced persons moved in with other branches of the family or with friends or neighbors. As was already remarked, displaced people are very likely to ignore the relief agencies. Statistics from World War II point to the same type of independent behavior on the part of disaster victims. Of the nearly 1,400,000 persons made homeless in the London region, only about one in seven passed through the official rest centers provided by the government. Six out of seven solved their personal problem in their own way. It is characteristic for families to move together, rather than as individuals.

But it is not only in obtaining temporary accommodations that disaster victims are capable of fending for themselves. They also work in small informal groups to cope with the most immediate problems brought on by the disaster. Thus, after a tornado in Flint, Michigan, with almost no aid from formal agencies, the victim and the fringe populations were able within three or four hours to rescue and transport to nearby hospitals over 600 of the 927 casualties.

Even in the most extensive disasters the formal agencies apparently succeed in making contact with only a fraction of the total number of victims. In working out their troubles, individuals may move quickly out of the impact area and the relief workers may actually have no idea where to find them. In fact, there is considerable evidence that, far from seeking aid, people turn to official disaster organizations only as the last resource. Ordinarily they turn first to their own families or close friends, next to church or other groups with which they are affiliated, then to other members of the community, even strangers—all before turning to the more impersonal formal organizations such as the police and welfare departments or the Red Cross and Civil Defense.

THE IMAGE OF "CONTROL"

A popular misconception often harbored by disaster authorities is that withdrawal from the scene of danger can be largely "controlled." It is, of course, the job of administrators to plan along these lines. But is this type of social engineering even possible? Quarantelli argues that it is actually extremely difficult for outside authorities either to initiate or to prevent withdrawal—unless they are totally indifferent to the reactions of the people involved.

Even totalitarian governments using compulsory measures during wartime are sometimes forced to back down and withdraw their orders in the face of widespread violations or violent objections. The British government was forced to change the rule which had initially banned the use of subway stations as overnight shelters from air raids during World War II because people persisted in using these convenient refuges anyway. Nor could orders prevent the nightly trek of between 30,000 and 50,000 people out of the English seaport of Plymouth when that city was under intensive bombardment by the Germans.

In short, when people feel they have a legitimate reason for not complying with regulations, official orders have no more effect on them than unpopular laws have on illegal gambling. Disasters, in themselves, do not necessarily make people more "controllable" than they normally are.

Naturally, expectation of the panic and dependency contribute to the belief that people in disaster situations will be pliable and easily managed. An additional ground for this viewpoint is the belief that social norms and values are transformed during crises. For instance, it is assumed that the values and prejudices concerning modesty, privacy, social class differences, intergroup relations, or self-reliance that individuals cherished before the disaster will suddenly be relaxed or break down altogether. It is thought that without these norms to guide them people will be ripe for direction from without.

However, all the evidence suggests that at most there is only a temporary and limited suspension of certain norms and values. Popular accounts of disasters often disguise this because they single out unusual happenings and present them as if they were typical of the victims as a whole. Journalists oftentimes play up the occasional looting that takes place after a devastating earthquake, an individual's temporary loss of religious faith when stricken (as was the case with Job, in the Old Testament) by tragedy, or the apparent breakdown in class barriers that seems to characterize life in an air raid shelter. But for the most part, people do not cast aside their fundamental values and customs.

Far from being in a condition of social disintegration, disaster communities, regardless of outward appearances and technical breakdowns, retain their social systems. These social systems continue to operate through all stages of the disaster. Under such conditions, it is impossible that outsiders could exercise more than partial control over the behavior of a community.

Furthermore, in Quarantelli's estimation, it would be highly inefficient for disaster populations to let the burden of withdrawing fall *exclusively* on relief agencies. The independent and striving behavior of victims represents the first step in their recovery from the disaster.

Hero Worship*

What new social types, styles, and ethical ideals are represented by the emerging heroes of today?

On the whole, is hero worship working to unite or to divide mankind?

What function does the hero fill in society?

To millions of Americans, the greatest of all popular heroes is still Charles Lindbergh, the man who made the first solo flight across the Atlantic.

On the day before his flight in 1927, Lindbergh sat unknown and unrecognized in a restaurant. Two days later, he had become the most celebrated man in American history. His feat touched off a flood of hysterical worship that lasted for several years and almost turned him into a demigod. He was officially recognized by Congress as a national hero and was paraded through the streets of every major American city. Ten million medals were struck with his image and a postage stamp was issued in his honor.

Lindbergh's rise to fame and fortune followed, on a grander scale, the classic pattern of the making of heroes in our culture. First, he was a relatively obscure man of modest status. Second, he came suddenly to public notice by a spectacular personal accomplishment. Third, a spontaneous outburst of hero worship came from the mass public before his achievement was officially or formally recognized. And fourth, almost immediately myths and legends sprang up about him; he was celebrated in art, song, story, and verse.

This has been the pattern by which scores of other popular heroes have been created in the past 40 years—from Jack Demp-

* Adapted from "Hero Worship in America" by Orrin E. Klapp, *American Sociological Review*, Vol. 14, No. 1 (February 1949), pp. 53–62. Reprinted by permission.

sey and Babe Ruth to Dwight Eisenhower and John F. Kennedy to the Beatles and Joe Namath. With the exception of figures such as Kennedy and Eisenhower, most of the popular heroes have been athletes and entertainers. Sometimes even men of rather trivial talents have won public attention because of some zany stunt or outlandish exploit.

Such heroes are still created today; however, the speed of events in the sixties and seventies seems to have shortened their reigns as popular figures. For example, the first astronauts who walked on the moon never experienced the long-lasting adoration the public gave to Lindbergh. Moreover, today's "youth culture" has produced a new kind of hero—the "antihero." * It sometimes seems as if the new breed of "great men" win popularity precisely because they do not symbolize the traditional values of older people. Thus, in addition to athletes and astronauts, today's new heroes include singing groups (the Beatles and the Rolling Stones), intellectuals (Marcuse and Levi-Strauss), film directors (Godard and Fellini), revolutionaries (Che Guevara and Malcolm X), and even movie stars who have been dead for years (Bogart and W. C. Fields).

Despite the changing character of today's popular heroes, the process of their creation hasn't changed much since 1930. It is still the public—the fans and the devotees—who elevate a man to the status of hero.

According to the sociologist Orrin Klapp, who around 1940 undertook a classic study of the types of popular figure, the magic moment comes when the public develops a very special feeling for a man. These public sentiments include endearment, tremendous loyalty, reluctance to criticize, faith in him, or near-religious veneration. But Professor Klapp discovered other elements in hero-making. These are described in what follows.

Once a public figure reaches the status of a hero, he becomes a powerful social force. His name and image serve as an inspiration to the public. He develops tremendous influence reaching far beyond his own field. The entertainer suddenly becomes "box

* See "Middle-Class Delinquency" in *Delinquents and Criminals: Their Social World* in this *Readings in Sociology* Series.

CROWD AND MASS BEHAVIOR

office" and heads up charity drives. The politician wins votes, makes money for his party, and draws support from all segments of the country. The athlete fills the stands, writes books about his exploits, and even sells products by giving them his endorsement. Later in his career, he may become canonized, commemorated, and officially celebrated. When he dies, his tomb may become a shrine, his fame and exploits may become legendary, and a full-fledged cult may grow up around his memory.

Of course, not all popular figures complete the full cycle which would elevate them to the status of heroes. Many of today's "rock" stars fade from memory as soon as their hit songs are off the charts. Politicians are forgotten once they are out of power. And athletes sink into obscurity after a batting slump. Yet the processes of hero-making and hero worship still can be seen in the careers of almost every popular figure.

UNOFFICIAL WORSHIP: UNORGANIZED BEHAVIOR

Most hero worship is unorganized, unofficial, and spontaneous. The most common form is the popular homage with which heroes are greeted. Spontaneous acts—applauding, cheering, hoisting on shoulders, blowing kisses, and throwing down snowstorms of ticker tape—all express the intense admiration of the crowd. When Lindbergh landed in France in 1927, thousands of people rushed his plane, dragged him from the cockpit, and excitedly carried him around and around the field. It was more than a half an hour before his feet even touched the ground. The Beatles were literally stampeded by flocks of admirers. Even lesser heroes are similarly treated. In the 1920s, whenever the gangster "Scarface" Al Capone appeared at the races or a football game surrounded by his 18 bodyguards, a thrilled murmur and often cheers came up from the stands.

With the physical gestures of homage go all the other spontaneous expressions of mass love: songs, stories, works of art, fan mail, and gifts. Moreover, the public is insatiably curious about its heroes. Magazines and newspapers do a lively business publicizing the minutest details of the public hero's daily routine. Indeed, the entire publishing tradition of the movie fan magazines was based on the adoration of Hollywood stars. Many of these magazines recently have shifted their attention to other popular figures, among them "Jackie" Kennedy Onassis.

Sometimes the heroes are embarrassed and annoyed by the familiarity and possessiveness of the public. People feel they own their heroes and have no qualms about committing the most outrageous acts to prove their ownership. Crowds paw, maul, manhandle, and caress their heroes. People try to push themselves into photographs and TV films with them. The heroes also receive proposals of marriage, offers of business deals, pleas for charity, and claims of kinship. So many strangers claimed to be relatives of Jack Dempsey that he was dubbed the "cousin of all Dempseys."

Imitation is another form of identifying oneself with heroes. Rudolph Valentino created the fad of sideburns and vaselined hair, just as decades later the Beatles touched off the rage for shaggy locks. Millions of small boys have tried to swing like Babe Ruth, skate like Bobby Orr, or pass the ball like Joe Namath. Sometimes people even impersonate their heroes, taking on the same character, dress, appearance, and mannerisms.

Souvenir hunters also hound the hero, tearing at his clothes and stealing his possessions as if they were trying to capture a piece of him. Lindbergh's plane was nearly destroyed by souvenir hunters. He rarely got a shirt back from the laundry. And he dared not lay down a hat or even a piece of paper for fear that it would disappear. Strangely enough, no hero worshippers ever consider this behavior theft. Rather they look upon it as natural and right!

The expression of extreme homage on one hand and extreme possessiveness and familiarity on the other is the paradox of hero worship. Homage is an act honoring and revering the hero. Possessiveness and familiarity spring from the need to identify with him. The public wants to place its hero on a pedestal—and then climb up beside him.

OFFICIAL WORSHIP: ORGANIZED BEHAVIOR

The more organized forms of hero worship include such formal honors as official ceremonies of recognition, presentation of prizes, special distinctions, medals, Presidential receptions, or

Most Valuable Player Awards. Usually these formal honors come after the spontaneous and unofficial recognition by the public. In other words, the masses first acclaim their heroes, and then the government and other organized bodies officially recognize them. For example, after the Beatles reached the height of their success and popularity, Queen Elizabeth honored them with a reception at Buckingham Palace.

Another form of official worship is commemoration, that is, the attempt to perpetuate the memory of the hero beyond his lifetime. Formal honors may create status, but commemoration tends to establish the hero as a symbol. Appropriately, the monuments and memorials to heroes are usually larger, more magnificent, and more unusual than those for ordinary people. A perpetual flame burns over the grave of John F. Kennedy; our national capital is named for George Washington; Lincoln's head appears on both the penny and the five-dollar bill.

Historic sites and relics associated with the hero may also serve to commemorate him. Babe Ruth's slum home in Baltimore is now a national landmark; the clothing and personal effects of our past Presidents fill museums; and the entire town of Tombstone, Arizona, is a monument to western badmen.

Finally, at some stage in the process of organized, official hero worship, a hero cult emerges. There is no definite line between the usual behavior of the public toward its heroes and the special behavior of the public toward its heroes in the cult form, except that cult worship is often more periodic and regular. In other words, a cult usually promotes annual devotions or celebrations of the hero on some important anniversary, such as his death. All of these celebrations—whether it be the nation-wide observance of Washington's Birthday or the solitary visit of a mysterious woman to the grave of Rudolph Valentino—are designed to make the hero "live again" in the minds of his followers and fans.

Cult activities often take many years to develop. Thus it is difficult to imagine what status current heroes such as Joe Namath or the Beatles will have in the future. However, the yearly pilgrimages made by thousands to the grave of John F. Kennedy indicate that his memory has already inspired a cult. The revival of interest in the films of Humphrey Bogart and W. C. Fields is another example of the cult phenomenon. (Oddly enough, many of the cult members are too young to remember Bogart or Fields alive.)

THE IDEALIZED IMAGE OF THE HERO

All hero worship involves excessive devotion, with the result that the hero often becomes bigger than life. His personality is exaggerated, his virtues are magnified, and his powers are over-rated. Strangely enough, these myths about his greatness seem to spring up almost immediately, not with the passage of time or after his death. As soon as Lindbergh landed in France legends developed about his childhood, his ancestry, what he said when he got out of the plane, how he flew the mails, and a score of other exploits from the past, all demonstrating his courage, modesty, and kindness.

Similar myths develop about all heroes: Babe Ruth's ability to "call" home runs; Dempsey's tremendous strength; the generosity of Al Capone; the drinking bouts of W. C. Fields; the "death" of the Beatles' Paul McCartney. Each generation has its own heroes and myths.

All these exaggerations, interpretations, and tall stories are told and retold. Eventually, they create the mythical character of the hero. He emerges as superhuman. In short, illusion and myth are essential to hero worship—and are probably a major explanation of it.

Of course, a hero cannot always live up to his legend. The image of the shy, modest Lindbergh was altered by his feud with the press. Several reporters showed that he was actually unfriendly and downright rude. He lost public favor even more when he sympathized with the Nazi cause before World War II. More recent heroes have shared a similar fate. The legendary stature of Jackie Kennedy was diminished when she married Aristotle Onassis. And supposedly it was when they married that the Beatles began to lose ground as a major influence in modern rock music. Yet, despite disillusionment the legends persist; and most popular heroes manage to maintain some place in our cultural tradition despite the fickleness of the public.

THE ROLE OF THE HERO

It might be thought that the popular hero—because he is extravagantly admired, honored, and idealized—could easily achieve the highest and most important role in American society. Yet, even though he is often considered almost superhuman, he is not necessarily a leader.

Of course, many great political figures have combined the qualities of the popular hero with a talent for leadership. Certainly, John F. Kennedy falls in this category. General Eisenhower, too, was a great popular hero who was elected President for that very reason. In other lands, there are the examples of Churchill and de Gaulle, Nasser and Dayan, Castro and Kenyatta. Hitler, Franco, Stalin, and Mussolini combined these qualities to capture personal power. When an individual with great talent to attract the mass public commands authority at the same time because he holds high political office, he enjoys extraordinary power. More often, however, popular heroes remain only symbols. Men like Lindbergh, Dempsey, and Ruth achieve their status through individual skill, talent, or luck. They may excite, impress, and even influence the public, but they do not lead it.

If popular heroes occupy a special niche in the popular culture, what function do they fill in society?

First, most heroes are worshiped because they contribute to the general welfare, survival, or happiness. The man who flies the Atlantic alone blazes a trail for others to follow. The man who belts home runs out of the ball park thrills the crowd.

Second, heroes provide both inspiration and models for achieving fame and fortune. In a competitive society such as the United States, heroes are living success stories. They are often "poor boys who made good," achieving status through personal accomplishment. Thus, in the 1920s, Lindbergh was an inspiration for the sons and grandsons of immigrants who hoped to rise in American society. Today, black sports stars such as Willie Mays and Bill Russell offer the same inspiration for the young blacks in the ghettos.

Finally, heroes may serve as a rallying point for great groups of people with similar interests and goals. Current rock stars, for example, are common symbols and their music is a central theme in the large, loose population of young people known as the Woodstock Generation.

CONCLUSION

Hero worship is best described as a collective process by which individuals are selected, honored, and preserved as group symbols.

One generation may reward men for their saintliness; another generation may honor military heroism; and still another generation may revere athletic feats. One nation may reward bullfighting, another portrait painting, still another pearl diving. But, all through the hero worship of all generations and all nations run some common threads: unusual skill, great achievement, service to fellow men, and martyrdom.

In addition, hero worship seems to express the current mood and values of society. Therefore, the popular heroes usually reveal the people's special interests and concerns of that time. Lindbergh was a hero in an age dazzled by man's new discovery and mastery of flight. Today in the United States, when the "Establishment" is under fire and old ideas of achievement and heroism are being questioned, many of the youthful heroes are "anti-Establishment" figures: the Beatles, Abbie Hoffman, Jerry Rubin, Dr. Spock, W. C. Fields.

It is perhaps surprising that symbolic heroes exist at all today. With the public better educated and better informed, more sophisticated and more skeptical than ever before, it is remarkable that myths and legends can even find a foothold. Yet, the creation of popular folk heroes appears to be a continuing spontaneous social and political force.

The Riot That Didn't Happen*

Can theories of collective behavior be used in the management of a naturally occurring crisis?

By partaking in setting public policy will social scientists be able to learn facts about human behavior in emergencies which they would otherwise not know?

On Labor Day weekend, 1965, thousands of motorcyclists roared into Upper Marlboro, the county seat of Prince George's County, Maryland, for a national rally and races. The police were particularly uneasy because a few weeks before a similar motorcycle rally at Weirs Beach, New Hampshire, had turned into a nightmare orgy of drinking, burning, brawling, and battling.

But Labor Day came and passed in Upper Marlboro with only minor incidents. The expected and dreaded riot never happened.

The riot failed to occur partly because two young social psychologists helped to ease a potentially explosive situation. From studying the behavior of violent crowds, they had formed a general theory concerning situations which were dangerous or threatening. They worked in cooperation with the police at Upper Marlboro. Their antiriot tactics actually put the psychologists' theories to the test. Indeed, they demonstrated than an understanding of the processes of collective behavior together with cooperative planning by all parties can keep the peace.

More important, the Upper Marlboro story vividly showed that the role of the police may either prevent or provoke a riot. In short, riots do not have to happen. At the same time, the experience showed that the destruction and killing on our city streets and college campuses does not have to happen.

---

* Adapted from "The Riot That Didn't Happen" by Robert Shellow and Derek V. Roemer, *Social Problems* (South Bend, Indiana: The Society for the Study of Social Problems), Vol. 14, No. 2 (Fall 1966), pp. 221–233. Reprinted by permission.

EARLY WARNING

Social psychologists Robert Shellow and Derek Roemer of the National Institute of Mental Health first heard of the possible raid on Upper Marlboro by the "Hell's Angels" motorcycle gang from a police detective whom they had met in youth work. The scheduled motorcycle rally was then six weeks away.

At the time, police were uncertain how much truth was behind the rumors. The Hell's Angels are a California-based gang. The story that they might travel all the way across the country to "tear up" Prince George's County, Maryland, seemed fanciful. Still, the local area (Greater Washington and Baltimore) had its own gangs corresponding to the Hell's Angels. The authorities naturally were worried that these local cyclists might take matters into their own hands.

The two social scientists volunteered to track down the rumors and to judge the likelihood of trouble. They started by reviewing the facts known about other riots connected with recreational or sporting events such as motorcycle rallies. They learned that there is a set of conditions that may produce a situation leading to rioting.

First of all, there is the arrival of outsiders in a small town or small area. The outsiders usually outnumber the local inhabitants and law enforcement officers.

Secondly, the outsiders are obviously set apart from the local people by some common interest (such as motorcycling), or by some characteristic (such as race, or age—as in the case of "college kids"), or by place of residence (as in the case of urbanites who drive out to the country). Thirdly, the contrast between the local people and the outsiders is made sharper by differences, for example, in dress, hair style, or vocabulary.

The social psychologists also found that the normal high spirits, funmaking, or rowdiness of the outsiders can often explode into destructive rioting under the following conditions:

When recreational, service, or control facilities are grossly insufficient for the great number of visitors. In short, when the outsiders find themselves at loose ends with nothing to do, they are ready for any kind of action.

When police and local officials make ineffectual or provocative attempts to control the crowds. This might be, for example,

CROWD AND MASS BEHAVIOR

when the police harass people just because they "look weird," at the same time revealing to the crowd that they lack manpower to control the situation effectively.

When a strong sense of group identity and solidarity develops among the outsiders—for example, when the outsiders feel they must band together against the "straights" or the "pigs." Often, the local residents help unite the outsiders by openly referring to *all* as "punks," "bums," or "hoodlums" and treating them as such.

MEN ON WHEELS

The outsiders who congregated in Prince George's County in 1965 were a diverse crowd whose only common tie was their love of their "bikes." They came from all walks of life. And most were young. Most, too, were employed, as they needed to be, for a motorcycle with all its trimmings and extras may cost as much as $3000.

Motorcycle buffs claim that it is the size of the bike that separates the men from the boys. Those who own the giant Harley-Davidsons and the larger Triumphs and BSA's and who take part in the competitions such as races, field events, and hill climbs see themselves as a breed apart from the owners of Hondas and other lightweights. Many of the men and women who own the big bikes center their whole existence on motorcycling. They enjoy taking off on a moment's notice and riding from, say, Washington, D.C., to Atlantic City, New Jersey, to have a few cokes and snacks and return home before sunrise. These people regularly travel to weekend meets and camp out on the spot.

Like any hobby-sport, motorcycling has its formal and informal organizations. The American Motorcycle Association (AMA) is the largest official organization of bike riders. The clubs which belong in the AMA are "sanctioned" and governed by strict rules and regulations. There are also scores of smaller clubs which are unsanctioned and outside of the AMA which appeal to the more casual cyclists. These clubs do not enforce strict rules on noisy mufflers and "odd-ball" styling. Although most of them are merely informal and not necessarily lawbreaking at all, the AMA considers them all "outlaws."

In addition to the more or less conservative clubs, the "outlaw" class also includes the motorcycle gangs dedicated to general troublemaking. The Hell's Angels of California, the Pagans of Washington, D.C., the Devil's Disciples of Boston, and the Gooses of New York are among the more famous, or infamous, gangs. Spokesmen for the motorcycle "Establishment" describe them as the "one percent who cause all the trouble and give the sport a bad name."

The gangs, of course, are happy to be called One Percenters. They emblazon the percentage mark on their jackets. Long hair, earrings, German helmets, and greasy dungarees make up the rest of their uniform.

Regardless of their status as "sanctioned," "outlaw," or "gang," most motorcyclists are united on one point: they feel harassed by the police and disliked by everyone. Motorcyclists, as a body, consider themselves a persecuted minority among American motorists.

THE BIG WEEKEND

The Labor Day schedule included the "Ninth Annual Tobacco Trail Classic," a 75-mile race to be held on Sunday at the Upper Marlboro Track. This was the first time that the race had been AMA-sanctioned as a championship event. Famous riders were to be there to compete for points toward the national title. On Saturday, the day before the big race, lesser races were scheduled on the track.

At another track, 14 miles away in Vista, Maryland, but in the same police jurisdiction, field events (drag racing, riding the plank, sack races) would be held on Saturday and Sunday, and another AMA-sanctioned race on Monday. A dance hall was located on the track infield. Popular with Washington area blacks, the hall was to be open throughout the weekend for their convenience.

A crowd of between 3000 and 6000 was expected at Upper Marlboro. A much smaller, mostly black crowd was expected at Vista. Naturally there would be a good deal of riding back and forth between the two tracks, the campsites and recreation areas, and the taverns in between.

THE STRATEGY OF RIOT PREVENTION

On the eve of the rally no real evidence of an invasion by the Hell's Angels had been uncovered. Yet the possibility of trouble was still real. To cancel a major public event on the basis of a thin rumor was unwise. But the authorities could not allow innocent people and property to be jeopardized. Finally, officials decided to permit the rally. But at the same time they decided to take precautionary steps to head off any violence.

Working closely with police and motorcyclists, the two social psychologists laid down a strategy which they had devised in the light of their studies of riots:

First, they encouraged intelligent, sensitive planning for all the events and all the possibilities of the long weekend. They kept the mood sober simply by refusing to make wild predictions about possible trouble. Instead, the social scientists hoped to save the authorities from both headlong harshness and complacent relaxation by matter-of-fact attempts to anticipate the number of people, the activities, and the coordination of the local police in Upper Marlboro and Vista.

Second, they tried to avoid any polarization of police and motorcyclists. Polarization occurs when two groups grow increasingly aware of their special identity as separate groups, increasingly suspicious of each other, and increasingly likely to develop scornful stereotypes or offensive names for each other. Moreover, they feel more and more pressed to act as groups, even though initially they may have had only a single quality in common. Then there results a confrontation of "freaks" versus "straights," blacks versus whites, "radicals" versus "patriots," the young versus the old, and, as in this case, the police versus the visitors. To avoid polarization, meetings were arranged between local motorcyclists and civil authorities. Films about motorcycling were shown, and each group was given the chance to "air its gripes" about the other. By this technique, the two scientists hoped to show police that motorcyclists were not essentially different from other citizens and that, again like other people, they were individuals who could not be treated as a single group of "troublemakers." They also tried to convince police that harassment or indiscriminate harshness directed against a few cyclists could unify all the cyclists against them.

Working with the motorcyclists, the social scientists tried to involve the organized groups in the actual planning of the events. The cyclists were asked to police their own members, identify trouble spots, and inform police of major changes in schedules or of any large group movements from one area to another.

A third major goal was to make sure that proper facilities were provided for the outsiders. This would entertain them and keep them within the confines of the rally areas. It was essential that adequate and convenient camping facilities were provided.

The fourth goal was to monitor all the events of the weekend and to keep up a continuous flow of information to both the police and the rally headquarters.

EVENTS LEADING UP TO THE WEEKEND

As the day of the big rally drew nearer, rumors about the Hell's Angels grew wilder. Yet there was no definite proof that the Angels had planned anything or, indeed, had even left California. Instead, it appeared as if—in the eyes of the local motorcyclists—the Angels had become legendary champions who would come to the rescue of the oppressed if police got too rough. The great danger, of course, was that local gangs, such as the Pagans or the Gooses, might try to borrow the mantle of the Hell's Angels and become folk heroes themselves.

Despite this danger—and the advice of the social psychologists—the police never fully accepted the idea that local clubs should be involved in efforts to control the crowds. An exception was the club sponsoring the Upper Marlboro races. Convinced by the police that trouble this year might mean the cancellation of events in the future, the club agreed to set up camping facilities and to hire uniformed guards for the race track. The two scientists were also disappointed when the State Police publicly announced that they would "get tough with any rowdy-looking types." Later, however, they took a moderate stand.

However, there were some signs of positive cooperation. All county police were instructed to treat the cyclists just as they would any visiting motorists. More important, they were reminded that only illegal behavior—not style of dress, haircut, or bodily cleanliness—was a matter for police concern.

The social psychologists' program suffered a setback on Saturday morning. It was learned that the AMA club was not keeping its promise to provide camping facilities. Apparently it was unwilling to cover the expense of possible breakage and destruction. This meant the site originally planned for camping had *not* been rented for the weekend. Nevertheless, the first straggling band of arrivals immediately set up camp in the field across the highway from the race track.

This created a problem for police. The field was private property. They could not enter it unless the owner complained or a violation of the law occurred that could be seen from the road. However, if the police notified the owner about the squatters, he probably would ask police to remove them; otherwise, he would be liable for any personal injury on his land. At the same time, eviction of the crowd might turn into a small riot. Or it might scatter the cyclists throughout the county in areas potentially more dangerous to residences and businesses.

Fortunately the police used plain common sense. They did not notify the owner. Instead they decided to let the cyclists camp on the field as long as there was no trouble. The police continually drove by and occasionally stopped at the entrance. But no attempt was made to seal off or surround the place.

SATURDAY

On Saturday, only a few hundred spectators attended the scheduled lightweight and novice races at Upper Marlboro. Across the highway, however, hundreds more—both outsiders and local residents—conducted their own impromptu field games on the squatters' field. Actually, only a small proportion of these cyclists ever saw the 75-mile race or even entered the official track. Most arrivals came for the informal get-togethers, drinking, and excitement that go with such events—just as was the case at Woodstock, New York, in the summer of 1969, when thousands who came for a concert of rock music heard none of it but stayed on to enjoy "the sense of community." *

---

* See "The Flowering of the Hippie Movement" in this book.

Despite its ruts, humps, and holes, the center of the squatters' field became a drag strip. Groups, clubs, and even families set up camp in a crescent around the strip. The people at the far ends of the crescent wore conventional dress and hair styles and had expensive camping equipment. But in the middle of the crescent and at the head of the drag strip, a ragtag troop of One Percenters set up headquarters in a large tent with the red flag of revolution flying from the center pole.

Sullen young men and women milled around this command post. They wore nose rings, long hair, iron crosses, swastikas, and Halloween wigs and made menacing noises at any curiosity seekers. Most of them were in "Pagans" or "Gooses" jackets, although a few appeared with the distinctive "Hell's Angels" patch—a winged deathhead. In many cases the Angels' jackets did not certify actual membership in the gang from California. It is likely that the wearers of the jackets were local people who had bought them when on trips to California. They were trading on the fame of the symbol. Indeed, at no time during the weekend were more than 20 Angels seen; and no evidence was found of the arrival of reinforcements from the West Coast.

As the day drew on and the racing became keener, a group of short-haired local youths dressed in T-shirts and jeans tried to bring some order into the unofficial drags. One tried to flag each pair of racers to a start. He was fairly successful, until the enormous quantities of beer, wine, and liquor consumed by the racers began to take effect. His authority was slowly undermined. After a few hours, racers roared past him without waiting for the flag. Nonracers crisscrossed the drag strip and narrowly missed each other. As accidents increased, tension grew between the short-haired local riders and the long-haired outsiders. Finally, a fight broke out between a none-too-sober Pagan and a short-haired local boy. The latter punched the Pagan senseless, and then climbed on an auto hood and challenged the rest of the Pagans.

Joined by the Gooses and other One-Percenters, the Pagans charged the smaller local band. Just at that moment, however, a drunken cyclist fell off his bike in the field and was injured. Police along the highway saw the accident but not the fight and sent an ambulance and several cruisers to the field. The sudden coincidence of the arrival of the police startled the would-be combatants. The fight ended just as it was about to begin.

Then 20 Hell's Angels and Gooses set out for a local tavern for more beer. Just as they began threatening the owner, a police sergeant entered the bar. Backed up by three cruisers outside, he calmly asked the cyclists to leave. Impressed by his quiet show of strength, the cyclists did so without trouble.

Except for a few minor scuffles and some drunken episodes, no further incidents took place on Saturday night.

SUNDAY

By Sunday morning, some 300 motorcyclists had settled on the squatters' field. The unofficial drag racing of the previous day was resumed at a more frantic pace. At two that afternoon, a fire was set in a railroad caboose on a siding behind the field. Fire trucks quickly arrived to put out the blaze, but no attempt was made to find the arsonists. At three o'clock, someone started up a large crane at a nearby construction site and stole tools from its cab. At four-thirty (the time of the big race across the road) a young man removed the plates from his dilapidated car, set it afire, and drove it onto the drag strip with another sportsman riding on the hood. The car rammed a dragging cyclist who, like the rider on the hood, fell to the ground. Both broke a leg. An ambulance and a firetruck arrived immediately, and the spectators let them extinguish the car and carry off the injured.

Then, at six o'clock, the long-smoldering feud between the local cyclists and the outsiders finally erupted in a brawl. A ten-man squad from the Civil Disturbance Unit (CDU) quickly drove onto the field and dispersed the crowd. Half an hour later, however, a delegation of local motorcyclists went to the police and demanded the removal of the outsiders before "they took action in their own hands." Because the outsiders had broken no law, the police refused. The rival cyclists therefore continued to threaten and challenge each other as they milled about the field. Suddenly several men broke from the crowd, raced to their bikes and returned with bars, chains, and other battle weapons.

This time the police did not hesitate. The entire CDU poured onto the field and the men took up positions in riot formation around the crowd. The chief inspector drawled over a bull horn: "All right, men. You've had your fun. Now it's time to go home." That was all that was needed. Within 20 minutes, the area was cleared of all but some peaceful campers who were allowed to finish their dinners. No further disorder marred the activities in the County, at the Vista track, or at the nearby beach resorts on Sunday night. By Monday morning, it was obvious the threat of trouble had passed.

REACTIONS TO THE WEEKEND

Most civil authorities were satisfied that police had conducted themselves effectively. The County Commissioner, however, seemed to express a common opinion when he questioned why they had "to put up with the influx of motorcycle tramps who camp out, drink, and fight among themselves." However, some citizens pointed out that the cost of the extra police, estimated at some $10,000, probably would have been necessary anyway to pay for overtime traffic duty on a Labor Day weekend.

The cyclists themselves were generally satisfied with the treatment they received during the weekend. One spokesman claimed that for the first time in nine years of races he had heard none of the usual "atrocity stories" about police harassment. In fact, the local, short-haired cyclists involved in the fight thought the police had been too lenient.

CONCLUSIONS

There was no riot in Prince George's County. The citizens and their property emerged virtually untouched. The races were held. The outsiders camped, drank, and scuffled undisturbed for much longer than they had expected. And the full gang of the Hell's Angels never came.

Was all the concern, planning, and police preparation worth it? The social psychologists Shellow and Roemer think it was. The confrontation at the tavern, the crane incident, the caboose fire, and the brawling are all evidence that the potential for greater violence existed. Sooner or later, the so-called hoodlum element might have left the campground and looked for action elsewhere.

According to the social scientists, the members of the motorcycle gang need and seek out the stimulation of group action, excitement, and violence. They like to see themselves in the romantic role of outlaw.

Shellow and Roemer point out four factors which prevented the spread of violence at Upper Marlboro. The absence of these factors may be expected to lead to riot. The most important factor was the general police policy of firmness, fairness, and neutrality. Violations of the law were dealt with quickly and firmly, but motorcyclists were not harassed or deliberately provoked. The presence and availability of a strong force was demonstrated but not flaunted. Well-behaved cyclists—whatever their appearance—were not mistreated. Thus no one could use "police brutality," as a rallying cry. The police policy prevented the progressive polarization so often observed in troubled times.

The second factor was the decision not to interfere with the cyclists on the squatters' field. In the field, the potential troublemakers could be confined to a central, open area. They were free to come and go as they pleased, but could still be carefully watched. (In Chicago, the site of the Democratic National Convention in 1968, when Mayor Richard Daley refused youthful demonstrators a permit to rally in Grant Park, they were forced into the streets.) Moreover, the cyclists were allowed to do there what they usually do—drink, drag, and show off—without annoying anyone else. Keeping the crowd busy is important in preventing a riot. Most riots are preceded by a period of "milling around." Although the crowd seems to be aimlessly moving about during this period, its members are really exchanging rumors and facts and building up the energy and courage necessary for mob action.

The third factor was the continuous flow of information into control centers and back and forth between opposing groups. The meeting between cyclists and police before the weekend was most valuable. It helped break down stereotypes that each group had formed about the other. Thus each group was able to understand better the other's character and intentions.

Finally, there was the element of simple good luck. It was lucky that the potential rioters decided to remain on the campground rather than to roam the countryside; that an accident occurred at the same time as the first brawl on the field; that the rowdier cyclists chose to leave the field and the county immediately after their campsite was closed. Even the rivalry between the local cyclists and the outsiders was lucky, for it kept the two factions busy and prevented any alliance between them against the police.

Fairness, common sense, intelligent communication, and good luck prevented a riot at Upper Marlboro. Could they have prevented riots elsewhere in the troubled sixties and seventies? Perhaps so.

The element of luck certainly cannot be controlled. A chance remark, a blocked street, a misfired gun, an unavoidable accident, all can touch off panic in a crowd—or in a police unit. On too many occasions, however, it is not luck that is lacking, but the other elements of fairness, common sense, and communication.

Watts: Who Rioted and Why *

Does an individual need to experience immediate, personal contact with a mass social event in order to believe in an ideological interpretation of the event?

How accurate were the various believers in the "riffraff" theory which described the rioters as:
(a) a *small* minority of the ghetto?
(b) the criminal and irresponsible elements of the ghetto?

What seems to be characteristic of the rioters?

Did they have the support of nonrioters in the community?

How did the community interpret the Watts riot?

"Burn, Baby! Burn!" the short wiry youth screamed.

With this encouragement from one of its members, the gang of laughing, young black men, most in their teens and early twenties, swung around the street corner and headed for Foley's Appliance Store. Black smoke from a firebombed warehouse drifted overhead but did not seem to dampen the apparent holiday spirits of the young men. They skipped along like street dancers at carnival time in some strange war-torn city.

The stores on this street so far had been untouched by the rioting, now in its third day. But the large crowd of young women and older men gathered along the curb seemed ready for action.

The arrival of the gang brought a cheer from the crowd. In reply, the young men did little comic bows as they stopped in front of Foley's. His hair wrapped in a black bandana like some

---

* Adapted from "Rioting, Insurrection, and Civil Disobedience" by Ralph W. Conant, *The American Scholar,* Vol. 37, No. 3 (Summer 1968), pp. 420–424; also "Participation in the Los Angeles Riot" by David O. Sears and John B. McConahay, *Social Problems* (South Bend, Indiana: The Society for the Study of Social Problems), Vol. 17, No. 1 (Summer 1969), pp. 3–20. Reprinted by permission.

pirate's headdress, the short, wiry youth picked up a long piece of lumber from the gutter and stepped toward the plate glass. Swinging from his hip with a style like that of some baseball heroes, he took aim at the window. As he jumped back, the plate glass cracked, split, hung in midair for a moment, and then crashed to the street in a million fragments.

Led by the boy in the bandana, the gang swarmed through the gaping storefront. Within minutes, they reappeared, some laden with portable TVs, electric mixers, window fans, radios, and electric can openers. Several young men made a team to carry out refrigerators and stoves.

Most of the crowd simply cheered them on but several older men joined in the looting, or at least accepted "gifts" handed through the window. Seemingly out of nowhere, some young mothers wheeled up shopping carts and children's wagons to help take away giant color televisions and radio-phono consoles.

Only one black person—a clergyman whose church was on the same street—tried to stop the looters. He pleaded with them to return the goods and go home. The young men only laughed and the crowd ignored him.

Within less than 15 minutes, Foley's store had been stripped of everything portable. The gang of young men, each carrying some prize, moved on down the street to a new neighborhood. The crowd, too, drifted off to tenement apartments with its "liberated" merchandise—the spoils of war!

The looting of stores by large groups of black citizens was a common scene during the costly and bloody racial riots that rocked America's inner cities during the mid-sixties. Perhaps it was this disregard for personal property (much of it white-owned) that frightened the white community more than any other aspect of the rioting. Indeed, the widespread looting caused many white citizens to assert that the riots were only an excuse for criminals to steal without fear of being caught. This theory was largely untrue. Not only was it false, but it blurred the fact that the riots really were *group* actions and not the work of individuals.

Ralph Conant is a political scientist who studied rioting in a number of American cities at the Lemberg Center for the Study of Violence at Brandeis University. He describes riots as spontaneous outbursts of group violence marked by excitement and rage. The outburst of rage is usually directed against a specific state of affairs, a discriminatory practice, or any specific injustice. However, the typical rioter has no premeditated plan, purpose, or direction in mind in venting his rage. There may be individual instances of looting, arson, and assault during a riot and it may happen that criminals take advantage of the confusion. But according to Conant's analysis this is not the real reason for a riot. The riot and the rage arise as a collective, or group, response to a long history of suppression, frustration, and injustice. Any small event may touch off a riot—the arrest of an individual, the insulting remark of an outsider, or even simply the threat of harm— but the real cause is the general suffering of the group.

Both white and black leaders have tried to explain the real causes of the racial disturbances of the 1960s. Unfortunately, many white Americans still do not understand—or choose to ignore—the explanations. Instead, they cling to the view that riots are the isolated misdeeds of a few criminals. Perhaps this is the real tragedy of Watts, Detroit, Newark, and other cities which suffered violent outbreaks.

WATTS: THE MYTHS

The 1965 riot in the Watts section of Los Angeles was one of the most widespread and violent urban disturbances in American history. During the six days of rioting, 34 people were killed and 1,032 people were injured. More than 30,000 people actively participated as rioters and another 60,000 people were close spectators. Almost 1,000 buildings were damaged, burned, looted, or completely destroyed. The territory covered by the riot and sealed off by police was one and one-half times the size of Manhattan and larger than the entire city of San Francisco. The riot involved a population that was 80 percent black and larger than the population of Providence, Rhode Island. And, for three days, Watts lived under the strictest military rule ever imposed upon an American city in the twentieth century, up to that time.

Perhaps because Watts was the scene of the first and the most unexpected riot, it became a symbol of all the urban disturbances in the sixties. The pattern of events, actions, and conse-

quences at Watts was replayed scores of times later. More important, in Watts there were established two conflicting and contradictory "myths" about racial riots—one black and the other white
—which set the tone of later black and white confrontations.

Soon after the Watts disturbance, the black myth spread rapidly throughout the black community. It interpreted the Watts
riot as a genuine group protest over genuine grievances. Specifically, black leaders cited brutality by the police, racial discrimination, economic exploitation by white merchants, and apathy
and inaction by white politicians. This riot, as the blacks saw it,
was really an attempt to call attention to these grievances. It was
a message to the white community.

While a myth was developing among blacks that the riot
was a group protest, another myth was growing among whites. It
was just the opposite of the black myth. Obviously, if the black
version of the riot was correct, then the white community could
be held responsible for the unfair ghetto conditions. Thus, coun-
tering the black myth—and perhaps reducing feelings of guilt—
the white community developed the "riffraff" theory to explain
the riots. To many whites, the riot was caused by a small handful
of criminals who were only too glad of an excuse to steal, burn,
and kill. Uneducated, poor, unemployed, they were ready for violence. But, said the whites, the majority of "decent" black people
did not participate in the riot or support the actions of the riffraff.

SEPARATING FACT FROM FICTION

How does a sociologist or social psychologist evaluate two
such widely opposing myths and separate fact from fiction?

News accounts of the time were highly inaccurate. And
statements by politicians, both black and white, all tended to support some particular point of view. Two social psychologists, David O. Sears and John B. McConahay, and a research team at the
University of California at Los Angeles tested the validity of the
two myths by gathering accurate, detailed information on the
characteristics of the Watts crowd. Data on the numbers of participants, type of participation, and attitudes of participants about
the riot, would indicate how widespread black support for the
riot had really been. At the same time, the facts about the ages,

backgrounds, sex, and residences of the rioters might support or refute the white myth.

To conduct their study, the research team interviewed 710 Watts residents. The random sample consisted of 586 people who lived in the Curfew Zone and 124 men and women who were arrested during the riot. (The Curfew Zone was an area of more than 46 square miles sealed off by the police at the height of the riot. The Zone contains about three-quarters of the black population of Los Angeles and is itself 80 percent black.) Both samples of people were questioned by black interviewers who lived in the Curfew Zone.

RIOT PARTICIPATION

The interviewers used three means to determine the percentage of people who participated in the riot. Respondents were asked (1) if they had been personally active, (2) how many people they thought had been active, and (3) what events they had witnessed during the riots.

The most direct question was simply: "*Would you say you were very active in the rioting, somewhat active, or not active at all?*"

About four percent reported being "very active" and about 18 percent reported being "somewhat active." Thus a total of 22 percent claimed some participation.

The residents were also asked a more general question: "What percentage of all Watts people participated in the riot?" The answers indicated that most black people thought nearly 20 percent of their neighbors took part in some way. This was probably a very accurate estimate. It came extremely close to the 22 percent who had stated they took part.

Answers to the questions about what residents had seen—shooting, looting, stones being thrown, stores being burned, and large crowds of people—are in Table 1. More than half of the residents reported seeing the looting, burning, and large crowds, that is, the most visible public events of the riot. About one-fifth of the Watts residents also reported having seen shooting and almost one-third of the respondents saw stones being thrown. Obviously, the riot came close to the personal lives of a majority of the people living in Watts (Table 1).

TABLE 1

Reports from the Curfew Zone

EVENTS SEEN BY RESPONDENTS	YES	No	NO ANSWER DON'T KNOW, OR UNCLASSIFIABLE	TOTAL
Shooting	20%	67%	13%	100%
Stones Being Thrown	29	61	10	100
Stores Being Looted	54	40	6	100
Stores Being Burned	60	36	4	100
Crowds of People	60	33	7	100

KINDS OF PARTICIPATION

The psychologists expected that some of the 22 percent who claimed to be participants might really be people who had only stood on street corners and watched. Therefore they also asked direct questions about the kinds of things done during the riot (Table 2). The answers separated Watts residents into four categories:

1. *The rioters:* those who aggressively engaged in breaking windows, throwing "Molotov cocktails," shooting at police, and/or looting stores. About 15 percent of the sample admitted to these acts.

2. *The close spectators:* those who actually saw looting, shooting, and burning, but who claimed to have taken no part themselves. These individuals—about 31 percent of the sample—probably made up the large crowds of people cheering on the "rioters."

3. *The distant spectators:* those who claimed to have seen little criminal activity, but they did see some of the more visible events such as burning buildings and large crowds. About 27 percent of the sample fell in this group.

4. *The stay-at-homes:* those who claimed not to have seen anything. Only about 27 percent of the total population fell in this category.

TABLE 2
Participation in Rioting

Participants	Curfew Zone Sample	Arrestee Sample
Rioters: Said they took part, *and* saw looting, *and* burning, *and* crowds	15%	52%
Close Spectators: Said they did not take part but saw looting, burning, and crowds	31	26
Distant Spectators: Said they saw one or two instances of looting, burning, crowds of people	27	18
Stay-at-Homes: Said they did not see looting, burning, or crowds of people	27	4
Total	100	100
Total Number *	(523)	(116)

* Note: The number of cases here is 523 and 116, respectively. The remainder of each sample—63 and 8, respectively—is not considered because some data are missing.

NUMBER OF RIOTERS

The actual number of people participating in the riot (not percentages) has been a very controversial figure. The numbers supplied by civil authorities and newsmen are largely inaccurate and contradictory. However, more scientific tabulations have been difficult to make because the Curfew Zone was not a standard census tract. Also the Zone contained many migrants and its outer edges had neighborhoods whose composition was changing from white to black. Despite the somewhat uncertain population, the research team estimated that 200,615 blacks aged 15 and over lived in the Curfew Zone at the time of the riot. On the basis of the percentages given by blacks themselves, this would mean that between 31,000 and 35,000 people were "rioters" and between 64,000 and 72,000 people were "close spectators" of the Watts riot.

Black Perception of the Riot's Size

Although the Watts riot was certainly widespread, property was actually destroyed on only a few main streets. Still, most people imagined that rioting took place right in their own backyards. More than 15 percent of the residents claimed that in their neighborhoods rioters had been "very active." Another 37 percent said that in their neighborhoods rioters had been "somewhat active." Of course, those who admitted personal participation in the riot usually felt their neighborhoods were the most active. But, at the same time, nearly 43 percent of the people who had not participated also felt their neighborhoods had been active. In short, the riot was a very close, very real, and very personal experience for most people in Watts.

Attitudes Toward the Riot

As might be expected, the "rioters" usually made more favorable comments about the riot and were more optimistic about its results than any other group. The "close spectators" were a little less enthusiastic about the riot but were still highly optimistic about its effects. They often said, for example, that they disliked what had happened but felt it would at least make whites pay more attention to blacks.

The Watts residents were also asked:

Was the riot a black protest?
Did it have a purpose?
What was its cause?
Were the shops and businesses destroyed selected on purpose?
Were they owned by whites who cheated blacks?

The answers to these questions were rated on a scale ranging from "black protest" at one end to "senseless destruction" at the other. This distribution of the replies showed that, overwhelmingly, Watts residents thought of the riot as a "protest with a purpose" rather than as a senseless act. Surprisingly, living near the site of the riot or taking part in it seemed to have little effect on answers. The "stay-at-homes" and the "rioters" had the same conception of the riot. The idea of the riot as a protest was not simply used as a justification of looting and burning.

174

THE RIFFRAFF MYTH

All the data gathered up to this point showed that the black myth about the riot had some basis in fact. Moreover, the data destroyed some major premises of the whites' riffraff theory.

First, the riot was not strictly the work of a small minority. A large number of people either directly took part in it or gave moral support to the rioters. In fact, even the black community itself did not believe the riot was the work of a small minority. By their own estimate, blacks thought at least 20 percent of the population had been involved.

The riffraff theory also claimed that the majority of "decent" blacks condemned the rioters. However, the data showed that a rather large percentage was either openly sympathetic or tended to condemn the civil authorities more than the rioters.

One last premise of the riffraff theory needed to be answered, however. According to the white myth, the Watts rioters were really odd, deviant, or unrepresentative members of the community. The rioters, said the whites, were the poor, unemployed, uneducated, and lower-class residents. The research team found that unemployed people living in ramshackle buildings tended to be more active in the riot. But this type of rioter played no great part. Instead, the disorder seemed to attract people of every sort —middle class, working class and lower class, educated and uneducated, employed and unemployed, alike.

Another version of the riffraff myth represented the rioters as recent immigrants to Watts who were unsettled and had no ties to their new homes. In fact, the research team found just the opposite: natives of Los Angeles were more likely to have rioted than were recent arrivals.

THE CHARACTERISTICS OF THE RIOTERS

If the description of the rioters as uneducated, lower-class, poor, migrants was incorrect, how then could they be described?

The research team found that the most distinguishing characteristics of the rioters was age and sex. Those identified as "rioters" were almost all young—68 percent were under age 30—and predominantly male. The "close spectators" were most often young women and slightly older men. And the "stay-at-homes" tended to be older people, especially women (Table 3).

TABLE 3
Participation in the Curfew Zone

PARTICIPANTS	AGE OF MALES			AGE OF FEMALES		
	15–29	30–44	45+	15–29	30–44	45+
Rioters	35%	10%	12%	20%	2%	4%
Close Spectators	23	38	31	40	26	26
Distant Spectators	22	32	26	18	36	31
Stay-at-Homes	20	20	31	22	36	39
Total	100	100	100	100	100	100
Total Number *	(75)	(78)	(86)	(111)	(80)	(77)

* Note: The total number of cases here is 507. The remainder of the sample is not considered because data are missing.

The significance of age and sex in determining riot activity was even more dramatic in the Arrestee sample (Table 4).

TABLE 4
Age and Sex of Those Arrested

SEX	AGE			TOTAL
	15–29 YEARS	30–44 YEARS	45+ YEARS	
Male	52%	14%	13%	79%
Female	11	7	3	21
Total	63	21	16	100

THE REALITY OF WATTS

From their interviews with the people in the Watts riot the research team produced a clear and dramatic picture of what happened—and why. Their scientific findings included the following:

1. About 15 percent of the population, or over 30,000 people, actively participated in the events of the riot. Another 30 percent, or more than 60,000 people, were close spectators.

2. The actual rioters were young men from all sorts of backgrounds, who were surrounded and cheered on by crowds of young women and slightly older men.

3. Whether actually participating or not, almost all ghetto dwellers were personally touched in some way by the riot. It was not an isolated and distant event viewed on television or read about in the newspapers.

4. Few people openly condemned the rioters. The majority of Watts residents agreed that the riot was a form of protest—"a message to Whitey!"

5. The white myth that a riffraff element was responsible for the riot was not borne out by the facts.

6. In general, the ghetto disturbance is a strictly local affair and most looters are "insiders." But even the looting of stores may be interpreted as a form of social protest. Related research done by E. L. Quarantelli and Russell R. Dynes suggests that all traditional ideas about personal property break down during riots. The looters, however, are not simply the "have-nots" or the riffraff who are trying to get something for nothing. Instead, the looters seem to be attacking the power structure which in their judgment has created an unfair imbalance in the distribution of goods to blacks and whites in this society.

All the evidence from Watts points to a situation behind the black mythology of riots. After years of being exploited by white merchants, persecuted by white policemen, and ignored by white politicians, the black community of Watts suddenly and violently erupted. Their riot was a message to white society.

Two Social Movements
and Their Fates*

When the circumstances which gave rise to an organization change or cease to exist, does the organization necessarily die?

How do organizations adapt to changes in their environment?

What possible changes may a social movement make in itself if it fails to attract followers?

When their situations change why do some movements change their doctrines while others do not?

What is the effect of changing environment on the internal composition of a movement?

The ball game was over and the crowd was pouring into the streets. A high-spirited boy with a bright headband bounded up from the sidewalk. In one big leap he gained the edge of the stone fountain. There he teetered, letting out loud joyful whoops. Then he caught sight of a group of five or six boys and girls and shouted to them to follow him. They all jumped up after him onto the fountain. Then, with the boy still in the lead, they dashed across the flower beds, leaving a trail of crushed geraniums in their wake. As if joining in a war dance, they pressed on leaping and howling to the nearby park. There they were lost to view in the crowd gathered around three guitarists.

A motorcycle gang appeared from nowhere and joined the

* Adapted from "Organizational Transformation: A Case Study of a Declining Social Movement" by Sheldon L. Messinger, *American Sociological Review*, Vol. 20, No. 1 (February 1955), pp. 3–10; also "Social Structure and Moral Reform: A Study of the Women's Christian Temperance Union" by Joseph R. Gusfield, *American Journal of Sociology* (Chicago: The University of Chicago Press), Vol. LXI, No. 3 (November 1955), pp. 221–232. Reprinted by permission.

178

clapping and singing throng. The crowd thickened. Soon there were high school youngsters, college students, boys and girls who worked downtown, and a sprinkling of dropouts, unemployed youths, and others, hard to classify—but all young and all for the moment with time on their hands.

This scene might take place in any American city, following any event that brings young people together. For outlets for their unfocussed energy they do not wait for big scheduled gatherings like the famous Woodstock Festival which attracted a third of a million youth in August 1969. What do they want? Where are they headed? Will their undirected force eventually concentrate upon some goal? And what goal?

There are no statistics, but neither is there any doubt that youth is on the move in directions as yet undetermined. Some organize to protest against the Vietnam war; others oppose pollution or the dress code set up by school authorities; some campaign for political candidates; and still others have not yet found a purpose. Some, like the flower children, seem to have come to an end. On the other hand, the Weathermen appeared in 1970 to be gaining power and influence. And in today's youth movement, this congregating and milling that follows rock concerts, ball games, and folk concerts plays an important role. For these occasions serve to bring restless youth together—to dance, sing, argue, and listen in the company of others suffering the same discontent as themselves. It was in this way that the Diggers, the hippies, and the members of communes in shacks in the country or "pads" in the cities found each other.*

Social movements often begin with just this kind of restless, seemingly random, searching. Then, more durable relationships may develop, goals are stated, leaders elected or appointed by themselves or the others, members assigned duties—in short, the movement may evolve into an organization. Many movements will develop out of the present restlessness of young people. What will they be? A social movement may have any one of a variety of careers and fates, as sociologists have discovered from studying similar phenomena in the past.

* See "The Flowering of the Hippie Movement" in this book.

The two movements which are analyzed here were large and often effective in their prime years. But they have gone out of fashion. One of them is apparently very nearly extinct. Because they are old enough to have a long history of ups and downs, they demonstrate some of the possible outcomes of a social movement. One movement was picked to show how it continued to survive under unfavorable conditions by changing its goals. The second movement held fast to its original purpose. But in doing so it lost its first friends and began to appeal to a different kind of member.

THE TOWNSEND MOVEMENT

Few people under 40 would recognize the name of Dr. Francis E. Townsend today. Yet in the mid-1930s, he headed a movement that claimed millions of supporters, had 2.25 million dues-paying followers, and was a very real force in American politics.

The core purpose of the movement was to relieve or prevent economic distress by establishing a pension for the elderly. Citizens over 60 years of age were to receive $200 a month. They were to be required to spend this amount in the United States within 30 days. Proposed during the depths of the Great Depression, the Townsend Plan and the Movement that supported it clearly reflected the concerns of that insecure era and touched a genuine chord in the hearts of many fearful Americans.

At its height, the Townsend Organization boasted 1100 clubs in the state of California alone. Today, it seems less real than the Bonnies and Clydes produced by that decade. After the Great Depression ended, the Movement lost momentum. The organization which it had spawned survived only by changing itself almost beyond recognition. By this course the Townsend Organization remained intact long after the mission which had brought it into being had been abandoned.

Sheldon L. Messinger, a sociologist at the University of California, Berkeley, studied the adaptations made for the sake of survival by declining social movements such as the Townsend Movement. His findings are described below.

The Townsend Plan, its supporters often said, was "not just another pension plan." It was a scheme designed to provide jobs

CROWD AND MASS BEHAVIOR

for the unemployed by keeping money in circulation and by enforcing the retirement of the pensioners. These objectives were a strength at first; later they became a difficulty to the Townsend Movement.

The passage of national social security legislation in 1935 struck a first blow at the movement by providing many of the country's aged with pensions. But this legislation did not completely undercut the Movement because the pensions were small (they are still below $200 a month), were not available to all aged persons, and, above all for Townsendites, seemed insufficient to end the Depression. More serious erosion of the Movement dates from about 1939, when economic recovery began. By the end of World War II, the Movement was struggling for life. By 1951 dues-paying membership had dropped 97 percent from the peak year of 1936. As prosperity increased, the Townsend Plan, devoted to ending depression, seemed increasingly irrelevant to most persons.

COMPROMISE AND CONCESSION

How did the Townsend Movement meet the challenge of dwindling popularity? Had the pensions for the elderly been the only Townsend goal its task might have been simpler. But from the beginning the Townsend Movement aimed at economic recovery through pensions. This, as we have noted, seemed less urgent by the end of World War II. Further, its specific "Plan" for achieving this recovery provided continuing difficulties. Thus, the Movement supported *national* legislation: it was not a *state* pension scheme. Further, it did not require an elderly person to be in financial *need* to receive the proposed pension of $200 a month; he needed only to be over 60 years old. Consequently, throughout the thirties, national leaders of the Plan actively campaigned against any proposal for old-age assistance if it was at the state level and if it was exclusively for the needy.

But by 1943, some Townsendites, fearing the loss of supporters, took a step which appeared to contradict their own principles: In California, for example, they entered a full-blown campaign for a state old-age pension scheme. This proposal did require "compulsory spending" and that pensioners "cease work"—

two special Townsend features; therefore Townsendites *could* speak of the proposed state old-age pension as a "first step" toward the national Townsend Plan. But the "$200 a month" so dear to the Movement was not mentioned. It was a heavy blow to the Townsend Movement when the state program was turned down by the voters of California.

Again in 1947, with membership at a new low and a rival pressure group successfully winning members among the aged, the California Townsendites were forced to support a plan put on the ballot by others. It was even further from the Townsendites' original goals. In the 1947 scheme, only the aged *poor* were to receive pensions and nothing at all was said of compulsory spending. This plan became law, but the law was later repealed. The Townsendites were in a quandary—not knowing what attitude to take to the repeal—since they had, only grudgingly, supported the proposal in the first place. In the end they reverted to their original position: Townsendites were for "national pensions," not "state aid."

THE SUBSTITUTION OF THINGS FOR IDEAS

How does a movement survive when its ideas are no longer attractive? How does it support itself when its failure to win followers leads to increasing financial difficulties? In its early, more successful days, the Townsend Organization's income had come largely from the small contributions of individual members. This was supplemented by the sale of pamphlets, Townsend automobile stickers, license plate holders, buttons, and other items. All these articles as well as dues required the purchaser to be committed to the cause.

By 1939, however, the Townsend Organization took to raising money by promoting a completely different line of "products"—among them, candy bars, cough drops, coffee, a variety of "health foods," and the highly successful "Dr. Townsend's Vitamins and Minerals." Townsendites were selling the pills on commission and earning by this means one-fifth of the Organization's total national income by 1951. But in the advertising of these products the Townsend Plan was not even mentioned. Money raising was now detached from promotion of the Townsend Plan.

The tendency to detach day-to-day activities from the original purposes of the Movement also showed itself in the regular meetings of the Townsend clubs. In the early hopeful days, politics had been the chief business of the clubs. But in the 1950s half-hour business sessions became merely the prelude to several hours of card playing or partying—the "real" business of the evening. Even the pot-luck dinners and weekly dances, at first specifically designed to attract new members, became merely social functions, for the leaders feared that propagandizing would only drive people into rival social groups and reduce sorely needed funds. The few stalwarts in every club who remained true to the original mission often ended as outcasts, criticized by the bulk of the membership for "selling the Plan too hard."

According to Professor Messinger, the Townsend Organization's adaptation to decline is typical of the process in many waning movements. In the early positive phases, when people are pressing for social changes, and these changes still seem possible, the concern of the movement's leaders and members is with doing whatever is necessary to translate this discontent into effective action. Real discontent is a necessary precondition if the movement is to form a distinctive mission.

When discontent wanes, or the purpose of a movement loses relevance, the movement's local chapters do not necessarily dissolve at once. They may live on—but with predictable consequences for the organization as a whole. An increasing lack of public concern for the original mission and a tendency to pay less and less attention to it will mean a loss of members and the end of effective recruitment. This in turn will spell financial trouble. The organization may adapt by changing its orientation. In short, to survive it may abandon the values which provided its reason for existing in the first place. In their stead, it may make mere survival an objective. We need not assume that either leaders or members *want* this to happen. They may be very unhappy (most Townsendites were in 1951) but may know of no other way to keep their movement and organizations alive.

Thus Townsendism *survived* long after its time had passed, but only at the cost of losing its "true" self. Many a social movement has suffered precisely this fate and it may be the end that is in store for some of the movements which today are vigorous and popular among young people.

THE W.C.T.U. IN ITS HEYDAY

Quite another outcome was the fate of the Women's Christian Temperance Union (the W.C.T.U.). Like the Townsend Organization, it has for many years been "a movement in retreat," a victim of changing conditions which left it far behind. But unlike the Townsendites, the ladies of the W.C.T.U. have clung tenaciously to their goal.

In contrast to the situation of the Townsend Movement, the discontent with American mores which fired the temperance movement and W.C.T.U. activism is, if anything, even stronger today than it was 40 years ago. Furthermore, W.C.T.U. membership has not declined substantially from its all-time high during the early 1930s. Yet, despite these apparent signs of strength, the Movement is often described as no longer a vital force in American life. And, appearances to the contrary, it is not at all the same organization it was in its heyday.

How did the W.C.T.U. react to the change in attitudes toward drinking? Did the toleration of "Demon Rum" which has characterized American society since the repeal of Prohibition affect the organization's goals, values, or composition? These are the questions asked by Joseph R. Gusfield, a sociologist at the University of Illinois, who shares Messinger's interest in the adaptation of movements and organizations to transformed environments. To answer the questions, he first surveyed the history of the temperance movement.

During the nineteenth century the American temperance movement was merely one part of a wide humanitarian effort to improve the lot of the poor and oppressed by elevating their moral and economic condition. The W.C.T.U. was active, for instance, in campaigns to reform prisons, to shorten working hours and raise wages, to abolish child labor, to win equal rights for women, and to bring about legislation for the protection of female workers. Later, during the first two decades of the twentieth century, it financed a huge Americanization project to help incoming immigrants to adjust to their new home.

From its beginning in 1874, the W.C.T.U.'s main concern was the excessive drinking of the poor, the foreign, and the working class in general. Temperance was not out of keeping with its other goals of social reform, because temperance was then widely regarded as the solution to the economic problems of the lower classes. By changing the habits of the working classes, the W.C.T.U. hoped to instill in them the virtues of thrift, industry, and self-control by which, it was argued, they could then raise themselves into the ranks of the respectable middle classes. When drinking among the well-to-do was criticized, it was principally because of the bad example their habits were supposed to be setting to the lower classes. This attitude corresponded to the prevailing spirit of the times and was not a peculiarity of the W.C.T.U.

After 1900, when the campaign to stop the sale of alcoholic beverages grew very active, the W.C.T.U. played down its humanitarian interests, though it did not forget them. Other reforms were subordinated to the major goal of enforcing moral conformity. This the organization finally achieved on a national scale in 1919, the "year of triumph" and the high point of its power and influence throughout the country. In that year alcoholic beverages were banned in the whole nation by the Eighteenth Amendment to the Constitution.

THE W.C.T.U. IN RETREAT

The political strength of the temperance movement in America was always greatest in the states with the largest proportions of Protestant and rural populations. But with the decline of the rural culture, both in the city and the country, the values of temperance gradually became less respected. After the repeal of the Eighteenth Amendment in 1933, the W.C.T.U. found itself in completely altered circumstances. A new middle-class stance in the United States began to exalt the qualities of sociability and tolerance and to disapprove of the rigid Victorian attitude toward drinking. And the middle-class churchgoing public were the bearers of this cultural change.

As a consequence, the W.C.T.U. lost many of its most influential patrons—the wives of upper middle-class professional and managerial citizens—who had once lent their talents and prestige to the temperance movement. To these women, the best educated and the most socially concerned, the members of the W.C.T.U. began to appear as prudish "old fogies" and ridiculous busybodies who wished to force their own views on an unwilling public and who simply refused to move with the times.

How did the W.C.T.U. respond to the new situation? There were three possible alternatives to choose from: it might have given up its past commitment to abstinence and embraced temperance, a doctrine of moderate drinking; it could have returned to some of its old social welfare projects or taken on new and more "popular" enemies, such as drug addiction or juvenile delinquency; or it could have maintained its traditional attitude, abstinence. This last course would be at the cost of forfeiting the support of the most powerful segments of the American public.

It was this third alternative which the W.C.T.U. chose. The choice, however, brought it into ever greater conflict with the middle classes, which thereafter became the chief focus of the Movement's wrath and indignation. Moreover, this choice carried it even further away from its traditional concern for the underprivileged. Finally, its insistence on the legal restriction of the sale of alcohol made it difficult for the W.C.T.U. to cooperate with organizations interested in curing or preventing alcoholism. In short, temperance, once viewed largely as a means to social and economic progress, had become an end in itself—and, more fateful, the only end of interest to the W.C.T.U.

Why did the W.C.T.U. not accommodate itself to the demands of the times? Professor Gusfield finds the answer in the changing social composition of the Movement. His study of state reports for selected years between 1885 and 1950 shows that the socioeconomic status of the local leadership of the W.C.T.U. had dropped substantially. For instance, in Connecticut in 1885, 46 percent of local leaders were wives of professionals, proprietors, managers, and officials; but by 1950 they composed only 31 percent of the leadership. The difference was made up by a corresponding increase in the percentage of women married to skilled and unskilled laborers. Fifty-four percent of the leaders in 1885 and 69 percent of the leaders in 1950 were married to laborers. In essence, the social base of the W.C.T.U. had gradually become the lower middle class and the lower class. Though temperance had been largely abandoned by the successful middle class, this basically rural nineteenth-century value had filtered down to the less sophisticated lower socioeconomic levels.

The desertion of the socially prominent from the ranks of the organization also explains why the W.C.T.U. can no longer afford a philosophy of reform. Such a position is only workable when it belongs to the socially dominant. However, far from having a stake in the status quo, which it might wish to extend to the less fortunate, the W.C.T.U. can aspire only to challenge the social mores of the dominant class and to impose its own in their place. In sum, the W.C.T.U. chose to retain its historic mission at the expense of both the spirit and the effectiveness of the earlier organization.

CONCLUSION

These two case histories demonstrate processes at work in social movements. The movement takes form as discontented individuals recognize and launch an attack on some scapegoat—the poverty of the elderly and the economic plight of the nation in the Depression, in the case of the Townsendites; the damage done to the poor by the evils of drink, in the case of the temperance movement. In time the discontented organize to achieve the goals they all wish.

But then they must accommodate their beliefs and their course of action to changing times. The Townsendites lost ground when Social Security relieved, to some degree, the money worries of the aged. Their organization survived by compromising with this reality. The W.C.T.U. stood its ground and remained by its first commitment. But in doing so the W.C.T.U. lost its first type of followers and was compelled to seek adherents of a different kind.

What will be the outcome of the movements astir among today's youth? What will become of the hippie communes, of the ecology and antipollution clubs, of the antiwar organizations? Will they repeat the history and experience of one or another of the many movements which have drawn together the discontented? It is interesting to speculate what fate will be theirs.

War Toys and the Peace Movement*

How did the war-toy craze of the early sixties originate?

How is popular demand for a product created?

How has the war-toy craze influenced our cultural values?

How has the antiwar-toy movement influenced our cultural values?

WHERE DID ALL THE SOLDIERS GO?

(A Play in Two Acts)

Act One: Christmas Eve, 1961, in the toy department of a big department store.

A gray-haired man, obviously a proud grandfather shopping for gifts, approaches a counter piled high with plastic rifles, grenades, camouflaged helmets, and tiny replicas of tanks, planes, submarines, cannons, and bombs. A huge poster over the cash register shows an American GI single-handedly destroying an entire battalion of small brown-skinned soldiers.

Salesclerk: Can I help you, sir?

Grandfather: Yes, I'd like to buy a gift for an eight-year-old boy. You know, something that's popular with boys this year.

Salesclerk: How about this, the "Small Fry's Flamethrower"—you can fill it with lighter fluid and actually set things on fire. Or this "Little Devil Fragmentation Grenade"—it goes off just like the real thing and sprays little chunks of plastic for yards in all directions. Or this "Gotcha-Baby Booby Trap Kit"—it even shows the kids how to rig phony bombs and

* Adapted from "War Toys and the Peace Movement" by Carol Andreas, *Journal of Social Issues,* Vol. XXV, No. 1 (Spring 1969), pp. 83–99. Reprinted by permission.

deadfall traps. And here's a very popular item—"The Sergeant Slaughter Sureshot Killer!" This pistol has soft plastic bullets filled with red dye so it really looks like you've shot somebody. . . .

Act Two: Same store, same characters, Christmas Eve four years later.

Salesclerk: Can I help you, sir?

Grandfather: Yes, a few years ago I bought a great toy for a young boy—I think it was called the "Maimer Landmine" and it exploded when you stepped on it. I'd like to get something like that for another young grandson . . . Do you still carry them?

Salesclerk: Oh, I'm sorry, sir. We really don't have anything like that this year. How about an electric train, or an auto racing set, or a game of "Monopoly"?

Grandfather: Don't you have any of those submachine guns with the real smoke and fire? Or those toy bayonets dipped in play poison?

Salesclerk: No, sir, but maybe he'd like a storybook, instead? Or a chemistry set? Or a baseball glove . . .

Grandfather: Where have all the war toys gone?

Salesclerk: Well, sir . . . uh . . . for some . . . uh . . . reason, they are not . . . uh . . . very popular this year . . . uh, uh . . . that's all.

Among the many successful protest movements during the 1960s was the defeat of the "military-industrial complex" in the toy industry by associations similar to Women Strike for Peace. These groups were composed of determined mothers with little organization and no financial backing. Nevertheless, they convinced the nation's major toy makers and department stores that war toys were bad business.

Even today, however, many businessmen refuse to admit that the peace movement had anything to do with the sudden and dramatic drop in the sale of war toys. Instead, they prefer to believe that the decline was just part of a normal business cycle. Yet all the evidence indicates otherwise: that the antiwar-toy campaign was very successful.

THE WAR–TOY CRAZE

The mothers' battle against toys of violence, as they began to be called, came right at the peak of a national war-toy craze. Carol Andreas, a sociologist at Oakland University in Michigan, made a study of the war-toy craze and the protest it called forth. What she learned is told in the pages which follow.

In the past, wartime has always inspired great sales of war toys. Although the United States was not officially at war in the early sixties, the Berlin crisis, the Cuban missile crisis, and American intervention in the Dominican Republic all created an atmosphere that helped start the upward surge in the sales of war toys. The nation's toy makers fed the trend with extensive advertising and publicity campaigns. During the summer of 1962 and again, in the spring of 1963, after a winter of war fever caused by the Cuban crisis, all the major toy makers predicted a tremendous demand for their product.

Most toy makers thanked television for the boom. Several very popular "combat" shows were on the air during the early sixties. In addition, according to one toy maker, the rerunning of old war movies further stimulated "the kids' passion for army goods." But the most important stimulus, said the toy experts, was the graphic news coverage of "the contained but colorful conflicts" which had broken out in many areas of the world. According to the manufacturers, children's tastes in toys—or at least boys' tastes in toys—are to some extent influenced by world events.

It was not only the news that strengthened the toy market. The Department of Defense sent out military experts from Washington and reportedly offered free consulting services to any toy manufacturers who wanted to produce authentic military toys. As an executive in a company manufacturing toys remarked, "We have been working in close contact for a number of years with local officials in our own National Guard and Reserves, as well as with military officials up through, and including, the Pentagon." According to a magazine of the trade, advice and suggestions were just part of the Department of Defense's program "to promote wide public understanding of its objectives and accomplishments."

190

Inspired by real-life events, stimulated by television's "combat shows," and clearly encouraged by the Department of Defense, the sales of war toys shot dramatically upward in the early sixties. Seeking to demonstrate the great spurt in the war-toy craze, Carol Andreas measured the amount of advertising for "toys of violence" in *Toys and Novelties*, a trade magazine distributed to the manufacturers, wholesalers, and retailers of toys. She then calculated what percentage of its advertisements was devoted to the objectionable playthings (Figure 1).

Figure 1 shows that the percentage of advertisements in the general category "toys of violence" more than doubled between 1961 and 1964–66. The percentage in the simple category "modern war toys" more than tripled between 1961 and 1964–65. (In 1966, the Batman craze apparently accounted for the rise in the "detective" category of "toys of violence." On the other hand, "modern war toys" lost some of their popularity in 1966, but they recovered in the following year.)

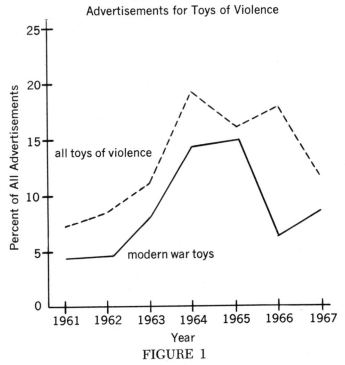

FIGURE 1

In response to this intense interest in war toys, many toy makers began specializing in them. Certain big companies turned over 70 percent of their manufacturing facilities to "war production." Retailers all across the country estimated that war toys accounted for almost 15 percent of the total toy sales, as compared with a rather stable five percent of sales before the craze. But even this figure failed to show the true extent of the craze, for perhaps 50 percent of all the toys sold for boys between the ages of five and twelve were in the "modern war" or "violence" categories.

THE RISING PROTEST

While American toy makers were turning into miniature military industrialists, a growing number of parents and educators were becoming more and more alarmed by the increasing popularity of war toys.

The scenes of warfare in Vietnam televised nightly across the land had encouraged toy makers to produce more and more realistic war toys; but the same scenes of conflict had turned other segments of the American population sharply against armed conflict. At about the time of the first peace demonstrations in the United States, an equally serious movement against the sale of military toys began to appear in many cities. In the fall of 1963 an organization of some 100,000 members called Women Strike for Peace began to distribute the news, ideas, and opinions of individuals and groups active in the antiwar-toy campaign in a publication called *Peace Education Bulletin*.

In 1964 and 1965 America's involvement in the Vietnam war increased. In 1965, an antiwar-toy publication called *The Toy* appeared. It featured articles, songs, and drawings by such influential persons as Jules Feiffer, the cartoonist; Margaret Mead, the anthropologist; Joan Baez, the ballad singer; J. Edgar Hoover of the Federal Bureau of Investigation; and Justice William O. Douglas of the Supreme Court.

Perhaps the most dramatic and effective protests, however, were the picket lines of angry mothers outside the big department stores and the boycotts of the toy departments. Obviously, these protests had an effect: they hurt the toy makers and the retailers financially.

THE TOY MAKERS' COUNTERATTACK

The first response of the major toy makers to this public criticism in 1963 was generally hostile and heated. The president of an important toy manufacturing company sought to justify war toys by pointing out that the United States had become a military society and that toy manufacturers could hardly be blamed for capitalizing on the trend. To counter the mothers' campaign, much of the toy makers' propaganda represented the antiwar-toy movement as a plot to undermine the security of the United States.

Of course, in part, the toy makers may have stiffened their refusal to heed the angry mothers. Most of the manufacturers had already produced their line of toys for the following year—and most of that line was military. One company, for example, reportedly had built "enough toy military vehicles to stock a motor pool." Another had backed its "GI Joe" line with expensive TV advertising. Indeed, in placing their orders for television advertising in 1964, all the major toy makers had anticipated a year of record sales.

Most toy makers continued their advertising campaigns into the 1963–64 winter season. The official spokesman for the industry, *Toys and Novelties* magazine, urged the manufacturers to strike back at the protesters. An editorial in the January 1964 issue implored the toy makers to answer "the vocal little groups of earnest, but misguided mothers who clamor so unrealistically against the production and sale of military goods as the 'teaching tools of violence.'"

THE MILITARY LINE CRACKS

Not all the toy makers, however, were willing to follow the lead of the military-industrial spokesmen, or to face the wrath of the indignant mothers. Actually, many toy makers saw the handwriting on the wall and began to reduce their sales promotion of military toys. One by one, the other toy manufacturers made similar decisions in response to the public outcry. Perhaps they realized that, after all, toys are still bought by parents, not by the young.

A final confrontation between protesters and manufacturers came at the 1965 Toy Fair, the annual preseason display of new toys held by the toy makers for the buyers of the major department stores. The manufacturers had hired psychologists to appear on television to defend war toys. But the psychologists changed their minds at the last minute and refused to cooperate. And the military experts from Washington who had previously visited the fair to help promote war toys failed to appear. The battle of the mothers versus the toy business' "military-industrial complex" seemed over.

Even the voice of the toy makers, the editorial writer of *Toys and Novelties* magazine, as much as conceded defeat in his editorial:

> What, after all, do toys really stand for? Diversion and entertainment . . . but much more importantly they indicate what skills we, society, think [a child] should develop . . . what vocations or attitudes or heroes he should glamorize. No one, I think, would give a child a game based on the activities of the Ku Klux Klan . . . or a miniature Nazi concentration camp. . . .
>
> What is required is that much deeper and more searching consideration be given to the values inherent in the toys [we] produce and sell.
>
> These values may well differ from those of marching mothers. But the underlying concern those mothers have for their children should be the toy industry's, too.

AFTER THE BATTLE

By the fall of 1966, the large department stores in almost every city where antiwar-toy organizations existed had been persuaded to stop advertising the war toys they already carried. Most stores adjusted their buying plans for the Christmas season to stock other types of playthings. Many stores even agreed to re-order certain popular war toys of past seasons only at the specific request of individual customers.

The influence of the antiwar protesters can be seen in the declining retail interest in war toys. It is shown in Figure 1 as the sharp drop in the number of advertisements for war toys after 1965. A similar drop in advertising was discovered by Carol Andreas in the number of pages devoted to war toys in *Sears*

Christmas Catalogs between the years of 1961 and 1966 (Figure 2).

Buyers for most large department stores in 1966 and 1967 reported that they had trouble even clearing their shelves of war items purchased several seasons before. Many toys previously offered in camouflage or khaki colors were repainted in bright colors and given themes not connected with war. And several of the manufacturers who had invested heavily in war toys faced bankruptcy or had sold out by 1967.

EVALUATION OF THE ANTIWAR-TOY MOVEMENT

It is difficult to evaluate the lasting effects of either the war-toy craze or the movement against it.

Certainly young boys still play at war today—and perhaps always will. Hundreds of thousands of children belong to the "GI Joe Club" and play out the adventures pictured in the club comics. And many American parents still feel that play with war toys is perfectly right and proper.

Pages Depicting Toys of Violence in <u>Sears' Christmas Book</u>

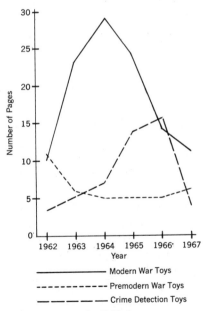

FIGURE 2

Because of this continuing, if subdued, interest in war toys and games, many businessmen argue that the marked decline in the sale of war toys after 1965 was really only a part of the normal business cycle. "One year war toys are hot," they say, "and the next year, medical or cowboy toys may be big." Yet the reaction against war playthings in the mid-sixties seemed to be deeper than the mere passing of a fad or fashion.

At the height of the war-toy craze in 1964, Carol Andreas made a survey in Detroit. She measured attitudes toward war toys among the parents of third- and fourth-grade boys. Her most significant finding was that all adults who said that their own parents had disapproved of war toys now discouraged their children from playing with war toys. In this case, at least, the modern parents showed no tendency to rebel against the attitudes of the generation which had preceded them.

The survey, made before the antiwar-toy movement gathered momentum, also revealed that most parents felt helpless in the face of the strong military influence in the toy departments. At the same time, they were uneasy about the moral questions raised by the survey.

The sociologists made a second survey three years later in the spring of 1967, after the peace protesters had gained considerable publicity. The same questionnaires as before were sent to the parents of third and fourth graders who attended the same school as the first group of children. The results were a blow to the theory that the declining interest in war toys was "a phase of the normal business cycle."

Almost the same proportion of parents in the second survey reported that their own parents had discouraged play with war toys. And all but one of these parents now reported having similar views about their children's toys. In addition, the overall proportion of parents who disapproved of war toys had increased from 37 percent in 1964 to 57 percent in 1967.

Moreover, a very definite trend toward peace was noted in all the responses of all the parents. No parents in 1967 approved of the use of tax money to support the makers of war toys, although about 16 percent had approved of it in 1964. Some 32 percent of the parents reported that they had not bought any war toys in 1967; it had been only 15 percent in 1964. Also in 1964 more than 20 percent of the parents had rated war toys and war games high on their lists of gift preferences, but in 1967 not one parent did so.

Obviously, the evidence is strong that the declining interest in war toys is more complicated than a simple change in consumers' tastes. Still, few toy makers will admit that the peace activists had *any* influence. They generally prefer to blame the reduced appeal of military toys on the general unpopularity of the war in Vietnam.

The peace movement's effect on war toys is only one instance of an oft-repeated social process.* It begins when individuals one by one respond in the same way, often in protest against something which they previously accepted. War toys, welfare department rulings, coats made of the fur of rare animals, or church or school regulations may cause the initial individual dissent.

Eventually, the aroused individuals find others of the same mind. At that point, speakers begin to give voice to the public protest, leaders emerge, and the interested crowd unites in an organization. The Women's Christian Temperance Union grew out of the protest against excessive drinking, and the inability of women to obtain divorces from drunkard husbands. Similarly, the antiwar-toy organizations developed out of antiwar protest. The collective behavior, that is the movement out of which all such organizations take form, is basically the same, no matter what inspired the protests.

* See "Two Social Movements and Their Fates" in this book.

The Women's Liberation
Movement*

What kinds of women are attracted to the Women's Liberation Movement?

Do they all join for the same reasons? Or does each kind of follower join for her own special reasons?

What objectives do all branches of the Movement share? Do the various kinds of members disagree on some objectives?

On August 26, 1970, over 25,000 New York women marched down Fifth Avenue behind the banners and slogans of Women's Liberation. To those who had barely heard of the Movement as well as to those who considered themselves thoroughly familiar with Women's Liberation, Women's Strike Day came as something of a surprise. There in the parade, proclaiming support for such "radical" programs as 24-hour child-care centers, free abortion on demand, equal pay for equal work, and an end to male domination, was not just a wild-eyed minority but virtually every kind of woman ever seen in the city—teenagers, telephone operators, waitresses, matrons from Westchester, Black Panther women, fashion models, nurses in uniform, Puerto Rican factory workers, and young mothers carrying babies on their backs. Miraculously, all appeared united, sharing their basic goals, enthusiasm, and, above all, militancy.

This scene, repeated on a smaller scale in dozens of cities across the country, served as public notice that "Women's Lib" was something more than merely burning bras or mastering karate chops. It was, of course, the more sensational ventures—

---

* Adapted from "The Rise of Women's Liberation" by Marlene D. Dixon, *Ramparts*, Vol. 8, No. 6 (December 1969), pp. 58–63. Reprinted by permission.

the carefully staged ogle-ins, the integration of traditional male refuges like the famous McSorley's Ale House in New York City, the infiltration of Atlantic City's Miss America pageant, and the picketing of the Playboy Club—which had most often captured the attention of the news media. The publicity generated by such events brought new adherents to the Movement.

Less well publicized, however, was the increasing activity of the women's organizations. It was showing itself in legislative campaigns to repeal state abortion laws and other legal disabilities of women, in the growing number of lawsuits brought by women against employers who discriminate on the basis of sex, in the mounting protest against the lowly position traditionally allotted to women in organized religion and the academic world, and in the indignant campaigns against the degrading image of woman continually presented by the mass media and the advertising agencies.

These campaigns, reinforced by the thousands of woman hours that have gone into "consciousness-raising," and informal discussions of why women are where they are and what they must do to win full equality with men, constitute the movement for Women's Liberation. August 26th, the day on which all branches of it joined together publicly to assert their claims and intentions, served notice generally that one more facet of the "American Dream" had collapsed—that American women, who for 25 years and more had been told that they were the most fortunate, the most privileged, and the most envied women on earth, were no longer "buying that package." Instead, they were demanding absolute equality and crying out, along with all the other underprivileged minorities, for freedom now.

The apparent suddenness with which Women's Liberation arrived on the scene, to say nothing of the intensity and passion of those converted to the cause, has puzzled many social critics. Feminism and women's rights, after all, seemed dead letters, part of a past, two generations ago, that evoked more humor than serious concern. Why, then, did they once again become burning issues in the second half of the 1960s? Marlene Dixon, a sociologist at McGill University and an activist in Women's Liberation, applied herself to this question. She arrived at the analysis which follows.

THE BEGINNING OF THE MOVEMENT

Women's Liberation, she explains, is related to the broader movement toward freedom that began in the United States in the early 1960s. Women have been swept up by that ferment, together with blacks, Latins, Indians, and poor whites—the whole second class of American citizens. As each oppressed group in turn discovered the nature of its oppression, so women began to discover that they, too, thirsted for free and fully human lives. The result has been the growth of a new women's movement. Its base includes poor black and poor white women forced on relief, working women exploited in the labor force, middle-class wives imprisoned in the split-level dream house, college girls convinced that sexiness is not the crowning achievement in life, and women of the political left forced to acknowedge that even in a freedom movement they themselves were not free.

The organizations that have emerged since the mid-sixties range from the nationally based, predominantly middle-class National Organization for Women (NOW) to local radical and radical feminist groups bearing such intriguing names as Bread and Roses, Redstockings, and WITCH. The new movement includes female caucuses—that is, small action groups—within every New Left group and within most professional associations and learned societies in the social sciences. Ranging in politics from reform to revolution, Women's Liberation has taken a critical look at almost every segment of American society and has constructed an ideology that rejects every hallowed cultural assumption about the nature and role of women.

What made women ripe for an independent radical movement? Certainly nothing in the decade immediately preceding the social upheavals of the 1960s suggested such mass dissatisfaction on the part of the "better half" of the population. For at least 15 years, from 1945 to 1960, the "feminine mystique" (the doctrine that women's happiness and fulfillment lay in home and family) had held undisputed sway throughout the land. Whatever problems women had were held to be purely personal and psychological, not social, while the few warning signals that appeared were either misinterpreted or promptly buried beneath an avalanche of praise for the American way of life.

The old women's rights movement had burned itself out in the frantic decade of the 1920s. After 100 years of struggle, women won a battle, only to lose the campaign. They obtained the vote and achieved a measure of legal emancipation but failed to destroy the real social and cultural barriers to full equality with men.

Then, for over 40 years, the movement was for all intents and purposes dead. Girls were born and grew to maturity virtually ignorant of the history of the rebellion of their own sex and of the true quality of the women leaders of the struggle, aware only of a caricature of "bluestocking" and "suffragette." Even though increasing numbers of women were driven into the labor force by the Depression of the 1930s and by the massive drain of men into the armed services in the 1940s, the old ideal remained: a woman's place was in the home and behind her man. Only these crises in American life gave women a temporary role outside the home.

When men returned to their jobs in factories and offices after World War II, women were forced back to the kitchen and nursery with a vengeance. It was the same old story once again: women, like blacks, have traditionally been used as a flexible, cheap source of labor under American capitalism. When labor is scarce, they are pressed into the labor market; when labor is plentiful, they are forced out.* They are kept at the bottom economically by low wages and the threat or actuality of unemployment. Without the opportunity to achieve economic equality with men, women's position remains a subservient one.

In the years after the war, the average age at marriage declined, the average size of families soared, and the suburban migration began in earnest. The political conservatism of the fifties was echoed in a social conservatism which stressed an almost Victorian ideal of the woman's life: selfless devotion to a husband and a houseful of children. Given the stamp of approval of "scientific" Freudian thought, this image of woman was an even more compelling force than it had been when backed by tradition alone.

* See "The Labor Force and How It Changes" in *Population Growth and the Complex Society* in this *Readings in Sociology* Series.

WHO JOINS WOMEN'S LIBERATION?

As the decade played itself out, however, three important social developments occurred which were to make a rebirth of the woman's struggle possible. First, women came to make up more than a third of the labor force; the number of working women grew to twice the prewar figure. Yet the marked increase in female employment did nothing to better the position of women, who were more occupationally disadvantaged in the 1960s than they had been 25 years earlier.

Second, the intoxicating wine of marriage and suburban life was turning sour. A generation of middle-class women suddenly woke up to find their children grown, while 30 or more years of housework and bridge parties stretched out before them like a wasteland. For many younger women the empty drudgery, as they saw it, in suburban life was a sobering contradiction to their adolescent dreams of romantic love and fulfillment as wives and mothers.

Third, a growing Civil Rights Movement was sweeping thousands of young men and women into a moral crusade, a crusade which harsh political experience was eventually to transform into the New Left. First Mississippi, then Vietnam, marred the American Dream almost beyond recognition. Millions of idealists were left with nothing but questions as to the worth of the most basic American institutions. Young Americans were no longer drawn to the suburbs. Instead, they flocked to Berkeley, Cambridge, Haight-Ashbury,° and the East Village, where traditional political ideologies and cultural myths—sexual mores and sex roles with them—were disintegrating in an explosion of rebellion and protest.

These three major groups which make up the new women's movement—working women, middle-class married women, and students—bring different kinds of interests and objectives to Women's Liberation. Working women are most concerned with the economic issues of, and are beginning to fight for, guaranteed employment, child-care facilities, fair wages, and an end to job

---

° See "The Flowering of the Hippie Movement" and "The Student Protesters" in this book.

discrimination, and in short, they are resisting their exploitation and are insisting that they be allowed to compete fairly with males in the labor market.

Middle-class women, psychologically handicapped by institutionalized segregation and an imposed sense of inferiority, are most sensitive to the dehumanizing consequences of a severely limited existence. Often well-educated and capable, they are rebelling against being forced to trivialize their lives. Many women feel they have lived only at second hand through their husbands and children. Many of them were crusaders in 1970 for the passage of the Equal Rights Amendment to the Constitution. But others do not want to see women treated like men, as the Amendment would require. They do not join the Movement.

Students, as unmarried middle-class girls, are most attuned to the issue of sexual exploitation. They have experienced the frustration of one-way relationships which offered neither the promised freedom nor any of the legal protections of traditional marriage. Young women have increasingly rebelled not only against passivity and dependency in their relationships with men but also against being defined in purely sexual rather than in broadly human terms.

The differences between the groups are, however, primarily those of emphasis rather than of fundamental goals. There is a growing understanding within Women's Liberation that all women suffer from economic and sexual exploitation and from psychological deprivation, and that out of their common protest may develop a powerful radical movement which crosses class and race lines.

WOMEN IN THE LABOR FORCE

Few would deny that women who work face exploitation and frequent discrimination. What is less well known is that their position when compared to that of male workers has actually worsened in the past generation. The gap between the two sexes has been growing wider, not narrower.

Though there are more women than ever before in the labor force, they have not been moving equally into all sectors of the occupational structure; rather, they have been shunted into the low-paying service, clerical, and semiskilled categories.* Unions which would work to further their interests are, of course, an essential precondition of progress; yet because male trade unionists have persistently ignored their needs, women remain essentially unorganized. Without support and organization, significant improvement in women's position is very difficult to achieve.

Not only are women forced into the lowest rungs of the occupational ladder, they are also kept in the lowest income levels of each rung. The most common injustice experienced by women is the income differential. While women might passively accept low-status jobs, limited opportunities for advancement, and discrimination in factory, office, or university, their indignation finally bursts out before the daily fact that the male worker next to them earns more—while often doing less.

In 1965, the median wage or salary for year-round full-time women workers was only 60 percent that of men, and that low figure itself represented a decline of four percent from 1955. Twenty-nine percent of working women earned less than $3000 a year, as compared with only 11 percent of the men. Only nine percent of the women earned $7000 or more as compared with 43 percent of the men. Furthermore, all women, regardless of race, are more disadvantaged than the average man, whether he is white or black. The earnings of white women, for example, are substantially below the income of males of either race. And black women, who bear the brunt of institutionalized inequality, earn even less than white women.

The occupational pattern is only reinforced by the declining position of women in the field of education. In the 1930s women received two out of five of the B.A. and M.A. degrees granted and attained one out of seven of the Ph.D. degrees. By the 1960s women accounted for only one in three of the bachelor's and master's degrees and one in ten of the doctorates. Furthermore, women lost ground in professional employment. There was, for example, a larger percentage of women on the faculties of universities in 1920 than in 1960. Clearly, then, the gap between the sexes has been growing wider.

* See "The Changing Lives of Women" in *Life in Families* in this *Readings in Sociology* Series.

CROWD AND MASS BEHAVIOR

MARRIAGE AND LIBERATION

Some women do not work, but most are—or will at some time—be married. And marriage as an institution has provided much of the grist for the liberationists' mill. Women differ from all other subject groups, so the argument goes, in that they are the only ones to marry and live on intimate terms with their oppressors. Yet it is through this very institution that the subjugation of women is maintained.

Why, then, do women marry? One answer lies in the economics of woman's position. For the most part, women are so occupationally limited that drudgery in the home is usually considered preferable to drudgery in the factory or at the typewriter. Secondly, women have no independent social status. In fact, as Marlene Dixon points out, there is no clearer index of the social worth of a woman in this society than the fact that she has none in her own right.

A woman is first defined by the man to whom she is attached but more particularly by the man she marries. She is defined secondly by the children she bears and rears—hence the anxiety over sexual attractiveness, the frantic scramble for boyfriends and husbands. Once she is married, her offspring are expected to supply her with some purpose in life and to endow her with greater social value through their attractiveness and accomplishments. Failure to have children is regarded as the same as failure as a woman.

But, ask the liberationists, what function does marriage perform in society today? Sex, love, child-rearing could, after all, be organized on a different basis. Marlene Dixon states that the housewife's role, usually defined in terms of the biological duty of a woman to reproduce and her "innate" capacity to give nurture and companionship, is actually crucial to industrial capitalism in an advanced state of technological development. For the housewife provides, unpaid, absolutely essential services and labor. In turn, her assumption of all household duties makes it possible for her husband to spend the better part of his time at work.

Yet the real productivity of her labor is denied by the commonly held assumption that she is dependent on her husband and gives emotional and nurturant services in exchange for her keep. This is because in a society based on commodity production, household labor and child care are simply not considered "real work," no matter how much energy or time they require. And since money determines value in our society, the fact that women function apart from the money economy provides the material basis of their inferior status. The vicious circle works like this: since their work is unpaid, it must be valueless, and because it is valueless, it cannot constitute "real work." Women who devote themselves to the role of housewife, therefore, are hardly worth as much as men who devote themselves to "vocations." Small wonder, then, that Friedrich Engels saw woman's position in relationship to man within the family as like that of proletariat to bourgeoisie, regardless of her status in the larger society. In other words, in all classes and groups, the institution of marriage functions to a greater or lesser degree to oppress women.

MALE CHAUVINISM AS A FORM OF RACISM

But if things are so bad, why have women not rebelled before? Even today, after the publication of numerous analyses and calls to action, many women disavow any sense of oppression and refuse to make the goals of Women's Liberation their own. This, says Marlene Dixon, is because women remain trapped in a false consciousness of themselves which is based on an acceptance of the concept of male supremacy.

Just as blacks were defined and limited socially by their color, so women are still defined and limited by their sex. It was once seriously argued that blacks were preordained by God or nature to be menials. It is argued today that women are destined to bear and rear children and to sustain their husbands with obedience and compassion. In fact, to many in the Women's Liberation Movement male chauvinism can only be understood when it is recognized that it is a form of racism based on stereotypes drawn from a deep belief in the biological inferiority of females.

In fact, the stereotypes used to justify society's oppression of women are almost identical with the images used to justify the oppression of blacks. For instance, the nature of women, like that of slaves, is depicted as dependent, emotional, incapable of reasoned thought, childlike in its simplicity, martyred in the role of mother, and mystical in the role of sexual partner. In its benevolent form, the inferior position of women results in paternalism; in its malevolent form, it results in a domestic tyranny which may sometimes be brutal indeed.

It took over 50 years to discredit the scientific and social "proof" which once protected the myths of black racial inferiority. Today most people can see that the theory of the genetic inferiority of Negroes is absurd. Yet few are shocked by the fact that doctors, psychiatrists, sociologists, and anthropologists are still busy "proving" the inferiority of women, or at least emphasizing the biological differences between the sexes in an attempt to justify the "separate but equal" treatment accorded women today.

Not surprisingly, the greatest obstacle facing those who would organize women remains woman's belief in her own inferiority, her acceptance of the "naturalness" or inevitability of her own status. Such a dilemma is not accidental, for society is geared to bring women to believe in and adopt as absolutely necessary their traditional inferior role. From earliest childhood to the grave, women are restrained and propagandized. Perpetually renewed by television, movies, and the women's magazines, the image of woman as "sexpot," "dumb blonde," "family drudge," or "frustrated shrew" becomes virtually the only image a woman has of herself. It is little wonder, therefore, that she may fail to rise above the image or that she can hardly imagine alternatives. Often she believes it—just as the blacks until recent years have accepted the doctrine of *their* inferiority.

What does this do to women? Psychologists have long known that black acceptance of white stereotypes leads to a mutilated sense of identity, to alienation, to rage, and to self-hatred. Human beings, it seems, cannot bear in their own hearts the contradiction of those who hold them in contempt. Marlene Dixon suggests that when women, like blacks, begin to turn their anger outwards, toward those persons and institutions which have degraded them and prevented them from becoming complete human beings, free to develop all their potentialities then, and only then, will they be on the road to psychic health, and then, and only then, will the American ideal of equality begin to be more than an empty promise.

It is still too early to say how great an impact the ideas and actions of Women's Liberation will ultimately have on society. But thus far the Movement has been gaining steadily in momentum. Women are no longer afraid that their rebellion will threaten their sexual identity. They are not frightened by their own militancy but are liberated by it. Much has been learned from the experiences of the antiwar and Third World movements and also from the failures of the earlier women's movement. The feminine mystique is no longer mistaken for politics nor is gaining the vote mistaken for winning human rights. Women in the Liberation Movement feel they are all together at the bottom of the economic heap, no matter what their social class or occupation, so that there is a genuine basis for a common struggle to win their freedom.

Suggested Reading

Each of the books and articles suggested here was selected because it sheds light on some aspect of unorganized behavior and adds something to one or several of the selections which make up this book. Many of them illustrate, for example, great chasms in opinion. Botkin's touching collection of old slaves' tales reveals how the human scene looks to the slave and how different his view of it is from the master's. Different in content but not wholly different in situation is the polarization of students and their "elders" at home and at school.

The greater part of the list consists of paperbacks on current themes such as black nationalism, student protest, and the hippie movement. Typical of this class of reading matter is a book written by a professional who is making a study of some social movement. The book is addressed to "the intelligent layman." Such a reader does not expect the profound or the technical. He may be watching or taking part in some event or process and simply wants to know more about it.

Books for the intelligent layman seem to be a growing part of the book trade. Perhaps it is growing because developments take place quickly today. It is hard to understand them even though they may be right under our noses. For, thanks to the cinema, newspapers, weeklies, monthlies, books, radio, and television—that is, to the mass media—we hear what goes on in a very wide world, too wide for the ordinary person to comprehend. Until recent years, books explaining real events were in the main about the past. But now the distinction between history—what did happen—and journalism—what is happening at the moment and still going on—is not clear-cut. Today books are published to explain the news while it is, if not hot, at least warm. As a result, at the very time when there are more demonstrations, more riots, more fads, and more instances of unorganized behavior of all sorts we can still be fairly well informed.

The few books of fiction on the list have been picked to stimulate imagination. William Golding's *Lord of the Flies*, for instance, depicts civilized boys in fear and panic "reverting to savagery." This is in contrast to the picture provided in the selection "When Disaster Strikes."

The greater part of the list is composed of scholarly research reports. These are not always easy to read but the main idea is usually plain. They have been chosen to confirm or to challenge findings reported in the selections.

Following the annotation for each title are numbers enclosed in parentheses. These numbers refer to the readings (see Contents) in this book, *Crowd and Mass Behavior*, on which they have a bearing.

Abu-Lughod, Ibraham, "The Mass Media and Egyptian Village Life," *Social Forces*, Vol. 42, No. 1 (October 1963), pp. 97–104.
Survey of the transmission of a piece of news through a village, showing how the educated learned the news by modern media and how it passed down until it reached the illiterate, largely by way of gossip. (4, 5)

Baldwin, James, *The Fire Next Time*. New York: The Dial Press, 1963. (Also a Dell paperback.)
Autobiographical essay on childhood in Harlem, leading up to his exposure to the Black Muslims and other black groups. (11)

Becker, Howard S., ed., *Campus Power Struggle*. Chicago: Aldine Publishing Company, 1970.
Collection of articles on student riots on Berkeley and other campuses and discussions of student aims and student power. (3, 10, 11, 12, 18, 20)

Bell, Daniel, "The Theory of Mass Society," *Commentary*, Vol. 22, No. 1 (July 1956), pp. 75–83.
Definition of mass society as one where people are in increasingly close communication and interdependence, yet have less intimacy, more concern over status, and a weak sense of identity. (2)

——, *The Radical Right: The New American Right, Expanded and Updated*. Garden City, N.Y.: Doubleday & Company, 1963.
A collection of papers by sociologists on conservatism, the discontented in 1955 in contrast to the discontented in 1962 and the social strains in those years, the John Birch Society and other extremist organizations. (13, 18)

Berelson, Bernard, "In the Presence of Culture," *Public Opinion Quarterly*, Vol. XXVIII, No. 1 (Spring 1964), pp. 1–12.
Research showing that the average American spends four hours a month on books, magazines, and the theater, of which 22 percent is devoted to TV commercials. (2)

Bird, Caroline, *Born Female: The High Cost of Keeping Women Down*, rev. ed. New York: David McKay Company, 1970.
Review of the changing role of women: their socially imposed handicaps, underpayment and insecurity of employment (which makes their plight like the plight of black Americans), discussion of their developing new roles. (18, 20)

Bogart, Leo, "Changing News Interests and the News Media," *Public Opinion Quarterly*, Vol. XXXII, No. 4 (Winter 1968–69), pp. 561–574.
Comparison of the importance of newspapers and TV as sources of news, showing that eight out of ten people read newspapers, six out of ten watch TV, and five out of ten listen to radio to get news. These ratios vary according to education; interest in a given item of news varies according to age. (4, 8)

Bontemps, Arno, and Conroy, Jack, *Anyplace But Here*. New York: Hill and Wang, 1966.
Study of the movement of blacks to escape the oppression of rural slavery or urban discrimination, usually by moving away but sometimes by "migrating across the color line," that is, passing for white. (7, 8, 9)

Botkin, B. A., *Lay My Burden Down*. Chicago: University of Chicago Press. (Also a Phoenix paperback.)
Collection of interviews with some of the last surviving ex-slaves, depicting their lives under white owners in the pre-Civil War South. (11)

Brink, William, and Harris, Louis, *The Negro Revolution in America*. New York: Simon and Schuster, 1964. (Also a Clarion paperback.)
Review of several movements in the black world, the role of the church, the new leadership. Contents include "What Negroes Think of Whites," "What Whites Think of Negroes," and "What It's Like to Be a Negro." (3, 5, 11, 18)

Broyles, J. Allen, "The John Birch Society," *Journal of Social Issues*, Vol. XIX (April 1963), pp. 51–62.
History of the society and analysis of its leaders and organization, its aims, the types of people who belong, and conditions under which it arose. (13, 18)

Carmichael, Stokely, and Hamilton, Charles V., *Black Power: The Politics of Liberation in America*. New York: Random House, 1968. (Also Vintage paperback.)
Explanation by its leader of black nationalism, with arguments supporting it. (5, 11, 18)

Crain, Robert L., "Fluoridation: The Diffusion of an Innovation Among Cities," *Social Forces*, Vol. 44, No. 4 (June 1966), pp. 467–476.

Findings based on surveys of political action revealing that the big cities lead in trying new things and that a city looks on experiences of a nearby city as an experiment, to be followed if successful. (5)

Davis, Fred, "Focus on the Flower Children," *TRANS-action*, Vol. 5, No. 2 (December 1967), pp. 10–18.

Interpretation of hippie values and hippie solutions to problems of marriage and family, consumption, poverty, and passive spectator sports as advance solutions to problems which society must face. (10, 12)

Drabek, Thomas E., and Boggs, Keith S., "Familism in Disaster: Reactions and Relatives," *Journal of Marriage and the Family*, Vol. 30, No. 3 (August 1968), pp. 443–451.

Survey made on the spot during the Denver flood of 1965, showing that the homeless turn to relatives and friends first for emergency aid. (2, 14)

Epstein, Cynthia F., "Encountering the Male Establishment: Sex Status Limits on Women's Careers in the Professions," *American Journal of Sociology*, Vol. LXXV, No. 6 (May 1970), pp. 965–982.

Description of the institutional barriers, one of the greatest being the professional organizations, which prevent women from entering professions despite educational qualifications. (11, 20)

Fanon, Frantz, *The Wretched of the Earth*. New York: Grove Press, 1965.

Rallying cry to the "Third World" of former colonials in the developing nations to strike for independence and nationalism and to repudiate European culture. (2, 11)

Feagin, Joe R., and Sheatsley, Paul B., "Ghetto Resident Appraisals of a Riot," *Public Opinion Quarterly*, Vol. XXXII, No. 3 (Fall 1968), pp. 352–362.

Report of inquiry among 200 blacks into their reasons for being on the scene after a riot in Harlem (New York) in 1964. (3, 16, 17)

Flacks, Richard, "Young Intelligentsia in Revolt," *trans* action, Vol. 7, No. 8 (June 1970), pp. 47–55.

Analysis of trends of the 1950s and 1960s among middle-class youth. These trends converged just when the population of young people was at its greatest and turned a small alienated elite into a mass radical movement. (12, 18)

Franklin, John Hope, *Color and Race*. Boston: Beacon Press, 1969. (paperback.)

Collection of papers by sociologists, anthropologists, and historians showing that there is racial prejudice throughout the world. (11)

Gilbert, Ben W., ed., *Ten Blocks from the White House*. New York: Frederick A. Praeger, 1968. (paperback)

Reporters' accounts of the Washington riots following the assassination of Dr. Martin Luther King, Jr. (11, 16, 17, 18)

Golding, William, *Lord of the Flies*. New York: Coward-McCann, 1962. (Also a Putnam paperback.)

Description of the behavior of a group of school boys on an island when social restraints are no longer effective. (2, 7)

Goode, Erich, ed., *Marijuana*. New York: Atherton Press, 1969. (paperback)

Collection of studies on drugs and drug use: motivation, effects, the connection between marijuana and heroin, the purchase and sale of marijuana; marijuana in the schools, the question of legalization. Much information on the drug aspect of the youth culture and the risks related to drugs. (7, 10, 12)

Grimshaw, Allan D., "Urban Racial Violence in the United States: Changing Ecological Considerations," *American Journal of Sociology*, Vol. LXVI, No. 2 (September 1960), pp. 109–119.

Comparison of black militancy before and since World War II in terms of the kind of neighborhood, the kind of violence, the locale of violence, and types of participants in violence. (2, 16, 17)

Gusfield, Joseph R., "Mass Society and Extremist Politics," *American Sociological Review*, Vol. 27, No. 1 (February 1962), pp. 19–30.

Definition of the political extremist as one who seeks to bar all who disagree with him from a share in the political process, to stifle discussion and to by-pass such institutions as the police and the courts. The mass society is able to tolerate some extremism and to accept social change. (2, 11, 13)

Hacker, Helen Mayer, "Women as a Minority Group," *Social Forces*, Vol. XXX, No. 1 (October 1961), pp. 60–68.

Definition and description of racial and cultural minorities, showing that women's situation is comparable; discussion of women's group identification and their status in various societies. (11, 20)

Horner, Matina, "Fail, Bright Women," *Psychology Today*, Vol. 3, No. 6 (November 1969), pp. 36–38, 62.

Report of psychological testing showing that bright women students try *not* to succeed. The author explains that women students are not socially rewarded for intellectual achievement. (20)

Hughes, Richard, *In Hazard*. Magnolia, Mass.: Peter Smith, Publisher. (Also a Signet paperback.)

Story of a ship caught in a hurricane and the behavior of officers and crew as the conventional holders of authority lost control. (2, 14)

Jack, Nancy Koplin, and Schiffer, Betty, "The Limits of Fashion Control," *American Sociological Review*, Vol. 13, No. 6 (December 1948), pp. 730–738.

Study of the reception of the "New Look" dress styles of 1947, showing that the average American woman will not follow the fashion if the fashion leaders attempt extreme changes. (6)

Jacobs, Paul, and Landau, Saul, eds., *The New Radicals*. New York: Random House, 1966. (Also a Vintage paperback.)

Description of the various organizations—for example, the SDS, the antiwar groups, and the communal groups, which have come out of the youth movement in the United States. (2, 10, 12, 13)

Keil, Charles, *Urban Blues*. Chicago: University of Chicago Press, 1966. (Also a Phoenix paperback.)

Description of the development of the blues and the importance of "soul" music to the black community, many of whose members are not inspired by civil rights leaders, but will trust and follow a blues musician. (3, 5, 11, 17, 18)

Kerckhoff, Alan C., and Back, Kurt W., "The Bug," *Psychology Today*, Vol. 3, No. 1 (June 1969), pp. 46–49.

Popular account of the research on social contagion reported in Selection Seven of this book. (7)

Klapp, Orrin K., "The Creation of Popular Heroes," *American Journal of Sociology*, Vol. LIV, No. 2 (September 1948), pp. 135–141.

Definition of the popular hero as a social type playing certain roles and appearing in certain hero-making situations. (2, 15)

Larrabee, Eric, and Meyersohn, Rolf, *Mass Leisure*. New York: The Free Press (A Division of the Macmillan Company), 1958.

Collection of studies on the spread of reading, sports, hobbies, holidays, and the uses of leisure among various social classes in mass society. (2)

Laue, James H., "A Contemporary Revitalization Movement in American Race Relations: The Black Muslims," *Social Forces*, Vol. 42, No. 2 (March 1964), pp. 315–324.

Account of the history, beliefs, and goals of the Black Muslims based on interviews with Malcolm X and others, interpreting the Muslim movement as an attempt among lower-class black males to develop a more satisfying culture. (11, 15, 18)

Laye, Camara, *Dark Child: The Autobiography of an African Boy.* (tr. by J. Kirkup). New York: Farrar, Strauss, and Giroux, 1969. (Also a Noonday paperback.)

Autobiography describing childhood among his own people and his eventual "white man's" education and westernization. (11)

Lomax, Louis E., *The Negro Revolt.* New York: Harper & Row, Publishers, 1962. (Also a Signet paperback.)

Analysis of the Freedom Rides, the sit-ins, and other forms of racial protest, also of the role of the National Urban League (NUL) and the National Association for the Advancement of Colored People (NAACP). (5, 11, 16, 17, 18)

McCord, William, *et al., Life Styles in the Black Ghetto.* New York: W. W. Norton, 1969. (paperback)

Report by four sociologists, black and white, who interviewed 1,000 city blacks and their daily routines and personal lives. (3, 5, 11, 17)

McGill, Ralph, *The South and the Southerner.* Boston: Atlantic-Little Brown and Company, 1963.

Account by the influential Atlanta editor of his own life and the history of the people of the South, showing forces that once brought blacks there and forces which now drive them out, and showing the whites as slave-owners, as Ku Klux Klaners, and also as supporters of liberty and civil rights. (7, 8, 9)

Malcolm X, *The Autobiography of Malcolm X.* New York: Grove Press, 1965. (Also a Dell paperback.)

Autobiography of the black leader describing his own conversion to Islam and the growth of the Black Muslims. (3, 5, 11, 18)

Marx, Gary T., *Protest and Prejudice: A Study of Belief in the Black Community.* New York: Harper & Row, Publishers, 1969. (paperback)

Reports of surveys and interviews revealing distinctive elements in the black population and challenging the white stereotype of "*the* black community", the meaning of black militancy; black attitudes toward whites and towards Jews. (3, 11)

Menninger, W. C., "Psychological Reactions in an Emergency," *American Journal of Psychiatry,* Vol. 109, No. 2 (August 1952), pp. 128–130.

Report of the behavior of victims and others during a flood at Topeka, Kansas, describing the nonvictims' impatience with rescue organizations and victims' readiness to make use of the organizations; victims' apathy and nonvictims' relief when actively engaged in rescue work. (2, 7, 14)

Moody, Anne, *Coming of Age in Mississippi: An Autobiography.* New York: Dial Press 1968. (Also Dell and Delta paperbacks.)
Life of a black sharecropper's daughter who after being a scholarship student, went into the Civil Rights Movement. (8, 9, 13)

Nordhoff, Charles B., and Hall, James Norman, *Men Against the Sea.* Boston: Atlantic Monthly Press, 1934. (Also a Pocket paperback.)
True story of the voyage in 1789 in an open boat of Captain William Bligh and 18 loyal men, describing the occasional tendencies toward panic and the captain's firm grip. (2, 14)

Nowlie, Helen N., *Drugs on the College Campus.* Garden City, N.Y.: Doubleday & Company (Anchor Books), 1969. (paperback)
Description (chapter 3) of the student culture, in which young people use drugs in group situations but for the sake of a highly individual reaction. (10, 12)

Quarantelli, E. L., "The Nature and Conditions of Panic," *American Journal of Sociology,* Vol. LX, No. 3 (November 1954), pp. 267–275.
Definition of panic as fear and loss of self-control, leading to nonrational flight. Such behavior occurs when the individual feels he is trapped, powerless, and alone in the crisis. Findings are reached after interviews on the spot with 200 people after an earthquake, a plane crash, and a dynamiting. (2, 4, 14)

——, and Dynes, Russell R., "Looting in Civil Disorders: An Index of Social Change," *American Behavioral Scientist,* Vol. 11, No. 4 (March–April 1968), pp. 7–10.
Interpretation of looting as black rioters see it—as a just and overdue redistribution of property with which many blacks who do not join in the looting are in sympathy. (2, 11, 17)

Rose, Arnold M., "Alienation and Participation: A Comparison of Group Leaders and 'The Mass,'" *American Sociological Review,* Vol. 27, No. 6 (December 1962), pp. 834–838.
Comparison of leaders of statewide organizations with a random sample ("the mass") of men and women, showing that leaders are better educated, less prejudiced, more likely to be in managerial or professional occupations, and more likely to be active in several organizations and to have more friends. (5, 6, 9)

Rosen, Harry, and Rosen, David, *But Not Next Door.* New York: I. Obolensky, 1962. (Also an Astor-Honor paperback.)
Account of the origin and organizing of protest by white residents in the face of rumors that black families were buying houses in their suburb; and of parallel organizing of residents who believed in desegregation. (2, 5, 11)

Sears, David O., and McConahay, John B., "Racial Socialization, Comparison Levels, and the Watts Riot," *Journal of Social Issues,* Vol. 26, No. 1 (1970), pp. 121–140.

Report of research on the background of the Watts rioters, showing them as Northern-reared blacks, accustomed to aggressive norms of behavior toward whites and suffering from a sense of deprivation. (3, 5, 11, 17)

Sellin, Thorsten, ed., "Women Around the World," *The Annals* (The American Academy of Political and Social Science), Vol. 375 (January 1968), pp. 1–175.

Collection of papers on lives of women in the United States, Canada, Europe, and some regions of Asia and Africa, showing changes in their roles, economic situation, education, and the laws affecting them. (20)

Shostak, Arthur E., *Blue Collar Life.* New York: Random House, 1969. (paperback)

Description (part IV) of blue-collar leisure and blue-collar voting. (2, 8)

Skolnick, Jerome H., *The Politics of Protest.* New York: Simon and Schuster, 1969. (paperback)

Chapters on historic political violence in the United States, the current protest against the Vietnam War, the student protest, black students, the "Third World" protest, black militancy, white militancy in the South (such as the Ku Klux Klan) and the urban North (such as the John Birch Society) and the role of the police in dealing with dissatisfied citizens' protests. (9, 10, 11, 12, 13, 17, 19)

Smith, Thomas S., "Conventionalization and Control: An Examination of Adolescent Crowds," *American Journal of Sociology,* Vol. LXXIV, No. 2 (September 1968), pp. 172–183.

Observation over five years of Labor Day riots of teenagers at a beach resort, revealing how leaders of cliques make use of these occasions to increase their own status. Riots tend to follow a pattern and eventually become conventionalized actions. (5, 10, 12, 17)

Spaeth, Joe L., "Public Reactions to College Student Protests," *Sociology of Education,* Vol. 42, No. 2 (Spring 1969), pp. 199–206.

Analysis of an opinion poll before the disorders at Columbia University, showing that the educated, the blacks, and the young reacted more favorably to the protest at Columbia University in New York City than the less educated, the whites, and the old. (2, 3, 5, 12, 19)

Vander Zanden, James W., "The Klan Revival," *American Journal of Sociology*, Vol. LXV, No. 5 (March 1960), pp. 456–462.

Analysis of the Klan's upsurge in 1955 after the Supreme Court's decision requiring racial integration in the schools and its return to inactivity when the integrationist movement was crushed in the Deep South. Largely blue-collar and lower-level white-collar workers, the Klansmen find support in ritual, racism, and super-patriotism, and thus make up for their growing feeling of insecurity in jobs and in social status. (2, 13, 18)

Westby, David L., and Braungart, Richard B., "Class and Politics in the Family Backgrounds of Student Political Activists," *American Sociological Review*, Vol. 31, No. 5 (October 1966), pp. 690–692.

Comparison of the radical left-wing students in Students for Peace and the radical right-wing students in Young Americans for Freedom, showing the former come from upper-middle-class Democratic families and the latter from working-class Republican families. (3, 5, 12, 13)

Westin, Alan F., *Freedom Now! The Civil Rights Struggle in America.* New York: Basic Books, 1964.

Collection of papers by outstanding scholars and activists on the struggle for civil rights, tokenism, prejudice in the courts and in law enforcement, and buyers' strikes. (12, 17)

Whitam, Frederick L., "Revivalism as Institutionalized Behavior: An Analysis of the Social Base of the Billy Graham Crusade," *Social Science Quarterly*, Vol. 49, No. 1 (June 1968), pp. 115–127.

Analysis of the big revival meetings showing that the audience is a distinct group, not a chance sample of the population. They are white, "old Americans," middle-class, already active members of established Protestant churches. (5, 7, 15)

Zurcher, Louis A., "Social-Psychological Functions of Ephemeral Roles: A Disaster Work Crew," *Human Organization*, Vol. 27, No. 4 (Winter 1968), pp. 281–297.

Study on the ground of volunteer crews of rescue workers helping survivors of a tornado which killed 17 in Topeka, Kansas, and made 2,500 families homeless, describing the crews' day's work and the changes in their roles as their work changed. (2, 5, 14)

Use of Paperback Readings With Various Social Studies Courses Other Than Sociology

Social Studies Courses

Paperback Readers	Modern Social Problems / Problems of Democracy	Urban Studies/ Growth	Family Life	American Culture/ Institutions/ Studies	United States History	Government / Political Science	World History/Cul- tures/Area Studies	Economics
Cities and City Life	1–20	1–20	1–3, 6–11, 14, 15	1–20	1–3, 7, 8, 11–20	1–7, 18–19, 20	1–3, 11, 14	1–5, 7, 8, 20
Life in Families	1–20	1, 2, 6, 9, 11, 12	1–20	1–14, 16–18	1–3, 6–14, 16–18	1, 2, 9, 13, 18	1, 2, 4, 5, 15, 19, 20	1, 2, 6, 18
Racial and Ethnic Relations	1–20	1–20	1, 4–9, 12, 13, 18	1, 4–18	1, 4–18	1, 2, 4–13	1–3, 12, 14–20	1, 10, 13
Delinquents and Criminals: Their Social World	1–20	1–20	1–3, 5, 7–11	1–4, 13–18	1, 10, 13, 14, 15, 16, 18, 19	1–20		1, 7–10, 16
Social Organizations	1–20	5, 8, 19, 20	3, 16	6, 9, 10, 17		8, 11	16	9, 12, 13, 14, 15, 18
Population Growth and the Complex Society	1–20	1, 2, 5, 7, 9, 18, 19	3, 4, 6, 16, 19, 20	14, 15, 16, 17, 19, 20	7, 13, 15		3, 5, 10, 11, 12	8, 10, 12, 13, 15, 16
Crowd and Mass Behavior	1–20	2, 11	3	4, 5, 6, 9, 10, 11, 12, 13, 15, 16, 17, 19, 20	8, 18	9, 11, 12, 13, 19		

NOTE: The numbers in the boxes represent the numbers assigned the individual readings, as shown in the contents of each paperback reader.

INDEX

Page numbers in italics indicate the first page of a reading by the author.

Interest groups, functions of, 15
Iroquois Theater fire (Chicago, 1903), 140, 143

John Birch Society, 135
Jones, LeRoi, 112

Katz, Elihu, 4, 7, *45*
Kennedy, John F.:
  as popular hero, 18, 148, 151
  reactions to assassination of, 1, 7, 34–44
Kennedy assassination:
  diffusion of news of, 36–37
  disruption of ordinary life caused by, 35–36
  effect on nation's beliefs and values, 44
  effect on public's critical judgment, 42
  first reactions to, according to respondents' color, region, and political bias, 37–38
  ideological interpretations of, 41–42
  NORC study of, 36–44
  physical and psychological reactions to, 39–40
Kennedy-Nixon TV debates:
  as a cross-pressure on Nixon supporters, 89
  effects on undecided, 87
  images of candidates before and after, 88–89
  limited effect on voters' final choice, 90
  relation to vote switching, 87–88
  survey of viewers' reactions to, 7, 87–90
Kent State, public opinion on, 138
Kerckhoff, Alan C., 4, 7, *69*
Klapp, Orrin E., 7, *147*
Kroeber, A. L., 7, *57*
Ku Klux Klan:
  backing by middle-class racists, 132

economic marginality of poor whites in, 131–132
  job competition between whites and blacks as factor in, 131–132
  and public opinion, 137
  working-class background of members, 130–131

Labor force, women in, 201, 202, 203–204
Lang, Gladys Engel, *1*, 1, 87
Lang, Kurt, 7, *87*
Lateral deviance, defined, 108, 109
Lazarsfeld, Paul F., 7, 79
Lindbergh, Charles, 147, 149, 150, 152, 153, 154
"Lost generation," 109
LSD, as used by hippies, 105–106

McCarthy, Joseph, 135
McConahay, John B., 5, *167*
Malcolm X, 18, 111, 115, 116, 118, 119, 148
Male chauvinism:
  effects on women's self-image, 207
  as a form of racism, 206
Marijuana, use by hippies, 105, 107
Marriage:
  age at, in postwar era, 201
  function of, in modern capitalist society, 205
  as oppressive of women, 205
  reasons women enter, 205
Mass behavior (*See* Collective behavior)
Mass man:
  described, 13–14
  factors in development of, 15
Mass movement (*See* Social movements)
Mead, Margaret, 23, 192
Menzel, Herbert, 47
Messinger, Sheldon L., 4, *178*
Methedrine, effects of, 106

Miller, Norman, *69*
Minutemen:
    frontier values of, 137
    guerrilla activities of, 136
    origins in post-World War II anticommunism, 135–136
    socioeconomic background of, 136
Motorcycle buffs, described, 157, 158
Myths, in social movements, 18

Nader, Ralph, 17
Namath, Joe, 148, 150, 151
National Advisory Commission on Civil Disorders poll, 28–30
National Negro Business League, 113
National Organization for Women, 200
Nation of Islam, 115–116
Nazi movement, 17, 18
Neighborhood defense leagues (*See* Urban vigilantes)
Nixon, Richard, effects of TV debates with Kennedy on, 87–90
North Ward Citizens Committee (of Newark), 130, 133, 134

Observation, as method of studying collective behavior, 6
Old-age assistance, 181–182
Onassis, "Jackie" Kennedy, 150, 152
Opinion leaders, characteristics of, 54–56
Opinion surveys:
    described, 95–96
    as method of studying collective behavior, 6–7
    sampling technique used in, 92, 96
Organization of Afro-American Unity, 118
Oswald, Lee Harvey, 39, 41, 42
"Outlaws," among motorcyclists, 158, 162–163, 165

Pagans (motorcycle gang), 158, 160, 162–163
Paramilitary rightists:
    and armed conflict against leftists, 135
    and John Birch Society, 135
    and Minutemen, 134, 135–137
Peace marchers (London, 1968):
    age of, 92, 94
    and anarchism, 97–98
    attitude toward authority, 97
    attitude toward violence, 93–94, 98–99
    influence of media and personal associations on, 92–93
    organization of, 98
    politics of, 93–94
    social background of, 92
    targets and goals of, 93
Peace movement:
    effect on war-toy industry, 188–197
    and London Peace March, 91–99
    and nonviolence, 5
    trend toward, 1964–1967, 196–197
Pensions, 181–182
Polarization, process of, 159
Police riot, in Chicago, 1968, 138
Population (U.S.):
    median age of, in 1970, 22
    percentage of blacks and whites in cities, 117
    percentage of youth in, 22
Prohibition, 184
Propaganda, defined, 15
Public:
    defined, 14
    distinguished from a crowd, 14
    and interest groups, 15
Public opinion:
    defined, 14–15
    formation of, 2

Quarantelli, Enrico L., 5, 6, *139*, 177

Committee on the Social Studies Curriculum of American Secondary Schools of the American Sociological Association

Neal Gross, *Chairman* (1962–71)

Harry Alpert (1965–67)
C. Arnold Anderson (1965–71)
Leonard S. Cottrell (1962–65)
Nicholas J. Demerath, III (1970–71)
Robert A. Feldmesser (1962–64; 1967–71)
Roy G. Francis (1965–71)
Lewis M. Killian (1965–71)
Paul F. Lazarsfeld (1962–71)
Bernard N. Meltzer (1966–71)
William H. Sewell (1962–71)
Gresham M. Sykes (1962–67)
Daisy M. Tagliacozzo (1968–71)
John A. Valentine (1962–71)
E. H. Volkart (1965–70)
Robin M. Williams (1962–66)
Everett K. Wilson (1968–71)

Sociological Resources for the Social Studies

Robert C. Angell, *Executive Director*

Helen MacGill Hughes, *Editor* of the
Readings in Sociology Series